T0157072

SURVIVING
A HOSTILE CITY!

Kent Alwood
and
Lorna Dare

iUniverse, Inc.
Bloomington

Surviving a Hostile City!

Copyright © 2011 Kent Alwood and Lorna Dare

All rights reserved. No part of this book may be used or reproduced by any means, graphic, electronic, or mechanical, including photocopying, recording, taping or by any information storage retrieval system without the written permission of the publisher except in the case of brief quotations embodied in critical articles and reviews.

iUniverse books may be ordered through booksellers or by contacting:

iUniverse
1663 Liberty Drive
Bloomington, IN 47403
www.iuniverse.com
1-800-Authors (1-800-288-4677)

Because of the dynamic nature of the Internet, any Web addresses or links contained in this book may have changed since publication and may no longer be valid. The views expressed in this work are solely those of the author and do not necessarily reflect the views of the publisher, and the publisher hereby disclaims any responsibility for them.

Any people depicted in stock imagery provided by Thinkstock are models, and such images are being used for illustrative purposes only.

Certain stock imagery © Thinkstock.

ISBN: 978-1-4502-7995-6 (pbk)
ISBN: 978-1-4502-7996-3 (ebk)

Printed in the United States of America

iUniverse rev. date: 1/7/10

Contents

You can't believe it – it really happened. A major disaster hit your city. No power, no phones, and you haven't seen a policeman in two days. Everyone is waiting around hoping that the Government will come to take care of them. But to this point there has been no help. You look out the window – there is a gang coming up your street looting house to house, and they are only three houses from your home! You remember talking to your co-workers and friends and family about what you would do at a time like this. You talked about the shows on TV and the movies and books that told about how you should be prepared, have food and water stored. But it's too late now. You will have to do with what you have …

You look at the street again, and now the gang is only one house away; you look back at your wife, daughter and little boy. They are so scared and looking to you to keep them safe and take care of them. You remember reading that during Katrina more than half the deaths were by gunshot, and 1,200 women were raped. What have you done so that you can save your family? Instead of buying food you bought a snowmobile and an RV? Well, you can't eat those, and they won't save you now. More important than that, what are you going to do about the gang out in the street when they get to your home? You are thinking, what can I do! We must hide or make a run for it! But where will you go if it is not safe out on the street?

Remember the time and money you spent on golf lessons? Well what you should have done was to have spent that time and money on training so that now you would have the skills and means to defend your home and family!

Does this scenario sound like you? How do you think this will end? Not well for you or your family? There is more to taking care of your family than just providing a home and a car. Don't put off the things you need to do to be prepared; you need to start now to get your life in order so that you can keep your family safe and alive in a disaster.

Surviving a disaster depends on you and your mind set. You and your family will survive only if you do what it takes to be prepared. Your family will live or die depending on what you decide to do.

This book is the first in a series of books to help you be prepared for a disaster. This book will cover many subjects that you need to know in order to survive. This book gives an overview of all the things you will need to know. Use this information to come up with a plan for yourself and your family to be prepared and have the ability to survive.

The next books will be how-to books, going into detail about the subjects covered in this book. Together, these books will be a library of life for you and your family.

In book II you will learn how to survive the situation described above. It may not be what is considered politically correct today, but it will be life and death correct. You will learn to be the predator not the prey. At the end of the day there can be only one winner. You and your family will live, and the bad guys will die. Or they will win, and you and your family will be dead. It is going to be up to you, what you do and what you spend your time and money on that will determine the outcome.

Book III will be dedicated to 72-hour kits and food storage. Book IV will cover survival medicine. Book V will cover nuclear, chemical and biological disasters.

Now is the time for you to decide and to act!

Prologue ~

How It Will Unfold

Government studies show how events will unfold in cities during times of emergency: most of the people who live around you will not leave at first. Many people will not have the money, transportation, physical health or ability to leave. Most will not have a place to go, and then many people will simply not want to leave their homes.

As food runs out and people see that no one is going to come and help them, they will begin to realize that they cannot survive where they are. They will be forced to leave with no plan or will try to survive on **the Hostile Streets of a City!**

Since 2007, for the first time, over half of the world's people live in cities. Cities are not made to be self-sustaining; everything needed to sustain the people must be shipped into a city. When the trucks stop rolling, it won't be long until the cities will be in chaos.

If you have food storage and are prepared, then you will not have to leave the safety of your home and go out into the dangerous streets. After thirty days, most of the population will have left for shelters or somewhere safe, and you will have the city practically to yourself as a resource to help you survive.

After the first thirty days when most of the population has gone, you will be relatively alone. Think of the city as a big supply house. Most of the homes will be abandoned, as will the businesses.

Remember what happened following Katrina. There was no food, and there were riots in the streets. One person was killed while fighting over road kill. In the Los Angeles riots, the gun storeowners were lying on the floor with AK-47's firing at anyone who approached. In New Orleans, people were shooting at the helicopters that were bringing them food and water. Those situations comprise just a small area of the country. Think how bad it will be if the whole country is in chaos.

Leaving to go into the countryside may sound like a good idea at first. You will remember all the farms, lakes and woods you passed on vacation, lots of space. Please realize that while country people do not know how to survive in the city, you will find it hard to survive in the country. If you do not have fuel and food, you need to realize that the people out there are not going to share with you. Also remember that it takes time to grow food and then to harvest and prepare it to eat. Even the people in the country cannot grow food in the winter, and most of the crops you see as you drive across the country are being grown to feed animals. This type of crop is not something you would prefer to eat. All that corn you see growing is not the same corn you eat out of a can; it is meant for livestock. If a disaster happens in January, it would be nine months before you could produce food to eat. The country people, therefore, will not be much better off than you are. If they do not have food storage so that they can survive until they can harvest the food, they will starve as well. The only advantage they have is that there is more game, fish and water available to them than to people in the city. People living in rural areas will have gardens, and most country people have guns and know how to use them. They will be more than willing to shoot city dwellers that come out on their land to steal their food. These people grew up with weapons and hunting. Weapons are a part of their lives. The ratio of city people with weapons to county people is 1 to 1,571. Think about it; how many people do you know who have and carry guns in your city, other then the gangs and criminals? Walk into a Wal-Mart in Angola, Indiana and try to rob it. You will find that a large number of the people in the store will be carrying guns. Most politicians in big cities make sure that the only people with guns are the police who will not be able to protect you. There will be no protection from the gangs that want to kill you.

Unfortunately, most of the people who live in the city will not be prepared and will wind up out on the streets or in the country fighting for their lives. They will find themselves doing things that are against everything they formerly believed in order to survive. Many will not survive.

Recently, thirty-three miners were rescued after more than sixty days trapped in a mine in South America. It was seventeen days before the rescuers were able to drill a hole to the miners to provide them with food and water. After the miners were rescued they each said that it felt like their body was eating itself, and that by the seventeenth day, they were thinking about eating anyone who died to survive. Without food storage you too may have to resort to cannibalism.

Food and water storage is critical to both your physical survival and your emotional survival. Without food and water storage you will survive physically only by committing acts you would never have thought of doing before a disaster happens. You may turn into a person you don't want to be.

Attention: Remember that trespassing, breaking and entering and stealing are illegal!

Even if there is a crisis, the city is abandoned, and there is no functioning government, laws will not be suspended. We are not telling you to commit crimes or break the law. We are pointing out ways to obtain food and supplies in a crisis. It is up to you to decide to what extent you are willing to go in order to obtain food and supplies. Allow us to reiterate again – remember that trespassing, breaking and entering and stealing are illegal!

This is another reason having food storage is important. You will not have to resort to high-risk operations in order to survive if you have enough food storage on hand.

Don't be a Victim!

When food, fuel and security are in short supply, what will you do? Will you be a victim or a survivor? How will you take care of yourself and your family?

If you are going hiking in the Rocky Mountains for a week, you need a good first aid book and a wilderness survivor manual – not this book. If your child falls off their bike, you call 911 and they respond, then you do not need this book.

This book is for those people who live in the cities and towns of America during a time when no one will respond to their 911 calls.

It makes no difference if there is a collapse of our finances, attack by terrorists, a plague, or a natural disaster; the end results are the same. You will be left alone to take care of yourself and your family.

What will you do without money, food, fuel, and 911?

With all of the uncertainty in the world and in the United States, it is time to be prepared to take care of yourself and your family. At a time like this when you may not be able to count on the Government to be there when you need it, a time when money may not be the staple it has always been, and there is no guarantee that your job will be there next year ...

You need to know what is in this book!

Foreword ~

The purpose of this book is to provide you with information and skills that will help you to survive over a long period of time. There is no religious or political agenda intended on our part, however, a strong faith and belief in a higher power has in the past, and does provide individuals and groups with an inner strength, courage and resolve to survive when others have failed to do so. This book provides skills for city and townspeople who may have to survive for a long time without outside assistance.

An emergency manual for an airplane tells you what to do if the wing comes off (the writer of the manual doesn't think the wing will come off and hopes that won't happen), but the airplane's safety manual tells you how to handle that emergency. So it is with this book. The things covered are what you will need to know for the worst-case scenario. We hope you will never need to use them, but it would be remiss of us to not provide you with this information.

This book will provide you with knowledge, but it will be up to you to decide if and when you will need to use this knowledge. Each person will have to draw on his or her own life experiences and beliefs to decide what to do with the information in the book. Again, we are not looking at the religious or political aspects in deciding what actions to take. That is for you to decide. For example, if you store food and want to share with everyone, that is up to you. If you wish to use a gun to protect your food and not share, that is up to you. We will deal only with the knowledge and means to store supplies, to help you survive.

If you decide to share your food, then you or your family could suffer. If you have to take a life to protect your food, then you will have to live with that. We are not trying to tell you to what extent you should go to survive; that is up to you. However, the better prepared you are, the better the chance is that you will not have to make those hard choices.

It will be up to you, based on your beliefs and life experiences, to decide what to do with the knowledge in this book.

Chapter One
Why be Prepared?

We are not predicting what may happen; this book is to prepare you for the worst-case scenario.

Why be prepared – because you are a Boy Scout? No, but like a Boy Scout, it is a wise person who is prepared to take care of themselves and their loved ones.

History has shown us what can happen to people, cities and countries that are not prepared for disasters. Some of you may think everything will be okay and nothing is going to happen to you. Some may think the worst that the United States is going to fall into total chaos. Most of you will fall somewhere in the middle. This book has information to help you be prepared no matter what your belief.

This book is designed to help people living in towns and big cities. There are many books and manuals available about wilderness survival. Many people will leave the city and get into trouble when they go to the mountains, or someplace where they are out of their element. They need a survival manual. The knowledge in this book will prepare you to survive in your own hometown when disaster hits where you live. It may be from a natural occurrence such as a tornado, hurricane, blizzard or flood. It may come from a terrorist cyber attack on the power grid. Or, it could come from a collapse of our financial system.

If a natural disaster occurs, you will most likely have to take care of yourself for short periods of time, from 72 hours to a week, and someone, most likely the Government, will be coming to your rescue. If a terrorist attack occurs, or a collapse of the Government or some of its agencies, then you may be on your own for long periods of time without hope that the Government will be coming to your aid in the near future.

When it is announced that a hurricane is coming or a blizzard, remember how quickly the local stores ran out of food. Keep in mind that most stores only keep about a 72-hour supply of goods in their stores, and that is at normal consumption rates. They rely on trucks to re-supply them on a daily basis.

We spoke to a high-ranking police officer in Chicago who said that the whole city is six meals away from a disaster. Most people only have food for six meals in their homes at any one time. The local stores only have a 72-hour supply of food. There are not enough police officers available to assist, and they would have all they could do to take care of themselves. This officer believed it would be just like the disaster in New Orleans where most of the police officers went home to take care of their families leaving the citizens to take care of themselves.

We cannot cover everything in great detail that you need to know in this book. If we did this, the book would be too large to carry. Think of this book as a guideline to help you know where to go, what to prepare for, along with a list of "how to" books you need to survive. There is so much information out there; you might want to make hard copies of some sources to keep on hand in case of a disaster when online information is no longer available. You may want to make a CD or a DVD. Or you might download information directly onto your PC or iPod.

We will try to cover the information you will not find in these other books such as ways to help the people in the cities who may not have the room to grow gardens and raise animals like people living in the country.

It is not easy to be prepared. To do it right you will need to invest a great deal of time and money. This will be worth it to you when the time comes and you and your loved ones are the only people around with food, supplies and the knowledge to survive when money cannot buy food. Every skill you learn and every precaution you take now can mean the difference between life and death.

You spend money on insurance for your home and car and for personal items. If you don't have a claim, then all the money you spent on the insurance is just gone. If you spend money on food storage, however, it will never go to waste. You can always eat it. Think of this as an insurance policy for your survival.

Besides this book you will need other books to be well rounded with survival knowledge and skills. You will need a good first aid book and a different book with information on food storage and cooking to get you started. It will also be of great value to you and your family to be trained on survival skills. There are many such schools out there. The Red Cross First Aid classes and the Heart Association can train you in Cardiopulmonary Resuscitation (CPR). The Church of the Latter Day Saints has extensive and free information on food storage. Make sure the people who are going to be around you also take this training. Remember you cannot perform

CPR on yourself, so make sure your friends and loved ones attend the classes too and pay attention; **you may need their help some day.**

You can take classes on survival at *pipehitterstactical.com.* They provide classes all over the United States on many survival skills; these are good training classes, because you receive hands-on experience as well as knowledge. If you are one who is going to obtain a weapon, then be sure **before** you buy a weapon that you receive some training on how to use it and what kind of a weapon you will need. In this book **(chapter on weaponry),** we will cover what kind of weapons you may need. The more you know and the more skills you have, the better your chance of survival.

The more you drive, the better your driving skill. If you want to play in a golf tournament, you need to practice and improve your skill. I am sure many people work hard at learning and keeping up their skills on games. Well, this is the **BIG** game. If you loose this game, you and your family could lose your lives. So, where should you put your time and money? Do you think that the people around you who are putting time and money into storing food and supplies while you are spending your time and money playing games, are going to share with you when the time comes? How about you? Would you share?

When disaster strikes, most of the people living near you will have to flee the city for food, and the city will be mostly empty within 30 days. If you have food storage, you will not have to go out into the streets and risk your life. After 30 days, you will have much of the city to yourself. There are many resources in a city that will be available to you when you are alone, but food and safety are your first concerns.

Most Important!

The most important thing about your food storage is to **Keep it a Secret!**

When you believe you need the information in this book and start to store food and supplies, you will want to share the idea with others. You will want them to understand and be prepared, too. Or you may just want to tell your friends about all the exciting things you are doing and reading. Whatever the reason, all we can say is **DON'T.** It will be a real temptation to tell people. Don't! It may be alright to tell people of your concerns about what might happen, give them a copy of this book and tell them you liked it or that you are thinking about being more prepared.

But **NEVER** tell anyone except the people who you intend to share your food and supplies with, the details of what you are doing or where your food and supplies are kept. This is the hardest thing of all to do and yet the most important thing of all to remember.

I'm sure you think your cousin who you grew up with would be a safe person to tell, or your best friend with whom you have been through so much. I wish that were true, but it isn't. Most of you think that your main threat is from criminals and the gangs on the street. They will certainly be a threat, but we have been all over the world and worked security during hurricane, floods and all kinds of other natural disasters. The gangs and bad guys will have weapons and no conscience for sure. What we have seen, however, shows us that the most dangerous people are the good people of the community - the ones who have worked hard and have been good citizens. When their children are starving, they will do anything to keep themselves alive. I know I would, and most of you would too. The gangs are a small number of the community, but all the people who live around you will be a part of the good people who also need to survive. They will be the biggest number and biggest threat to you. Your relatives who didn't listen to you and did nothing to prepare and spent their time and money on fun things, will now expect you to share your supplies and take care of them. At that point you will have to share what you have, and that means you and your family will do without. Or you may have to use force to protect your supplies. This is the reality you need to be thinking about when you consider telling anyone what you are doing.

If you tell people, then you will have to store more than you need so you can share, or be willing to use force, to protect your food and your family. These are not going to be easy decisions to make. You can avoid being in this tough predicament by keeping a closed mouth. Of course, there are people you will want to take care of and share with what you are doing. You will have to choose very carefully with whom you share this information. Make them understand how important it is for them to keep what you are doing a secret as well. It is hard for young children to understand and keep a secret, so keep that in mind.

Remember that this is the big game and whom you tell and what you tell could mean life or death for you and your loved ones.

Chapter Two

72-Hour Kit

In the United States, most families are six meals from disaster. You may think there is not going to be a long-term disaster coming, but everyone is in danger of short-term natural disasters such as floods, hurricanes, blizzards, power outages or tornados.

Everyone should have a 72-hour kit for themselves and each person in their family or group.

There could be a power outage, and you can remain in your home, or there may be a flood and you may have to leave your home with very little notice for a short period of time. You may have to relocate. You should scout out places that may be suitable for you to go. You may have a friend or family that you could go to for shelter. Make sure the people you will be going to understand you are coming, and make arrangements with them. You may be able to go to a Red Cross or FEMA shelter. You will find that most shelters supply only the most basic needs, and you will be ahead of everyone else and more comfortable if you go to a shelter with your 72-hour kit in hand.

On the web, in libraries and in bookstores, there is a great deal of material about what you may need for your 72-hour kit. Most of these sources do not take into consideration the age, health, size, religion and just plain personal preferences, of each person. So, we are not going to try to list everything you may need; instead we will give you guidelines as to what you should be thinking about when you put your kit together. These will be things that are specific to you and your family.

You can buy 72-hour kits on the web, and that would be a good start. These cost more than making your own, and if you do make your own, you can start it and add to it as you think of more things and as you have the money to do so. By making your own kit, you can personalize it to fit yourself and each person in your family or group who needs one.

If you have to relocate, try to let someone know that you are leaving and where you are headed. You should leave a notice with your name and a list of everyone with you and where you will be. Leave a cell number if you have one, the date when you left, and when you expect to return. Leave this note right on your door. This will assist the authorities if someone comes looking for you. Put your information in a see-through plastic cover to protect it from the weather, and secure it to the door.

Practice!

No matter how much you think and plan, you will forget something. After you put together your kits, you need to try using them. The first time you experiment, you should use your kits in your home and only for a weekend. Turn off all power in your home. Try to live using only your 72-hour kits to see what you have missed. You will be surprised what you still need. Remember to make a list and add it to your kit.

The second time you try out your kits, you should try utilizing your kits by going somewhere other than home, but not a hotel. Try a state park or someplace where there is no power. Also remember that if you have to leave, you need to address having fuel for your transportation to a safe place and have transportation that will accommodate you and your kits.

Appendix A at the end of this book has a list of things for you to think about including in your kit. Remember that you and your loved ones, as individuals, need to add things to accommodate your life style, culture and religion.

Water:
Remember you can go 30 days or more without food, but you will need water right away. A gallon of water weighs 8.3 pounds. That is a great deal of weight to carry around, so plan for that, as well. You will need two quarts of water per person per day just to drink. That is about 4 pounds per person for drinking plus any water you may need for washing, sanitation and cooking. Log on to *www.longlifefood.com* for more information or *www.pipehitterstactical.com* for training and gear.

Coming soon will be *Surviving a Hostile City III*. This book will be entirely dedicated to 72-hour kits and food storage.

Chapter Three

Food Storage

In this chapter we will talk about food storage, and in a later chapter, water storage. However, remember in subsequent chapters when we refer to food storage, we will be referring to both food and water as a unit.

Food storage is important to everyone in the United States, but it is more critical to people who live in cities. Country people have land to grow gardens and, as a whole, have larger homes with basements or crawl spaces and out buildings in which to store food. Hunting and fishing is more available for people living in the country.

Country people are more mobile. They tend to know and interact more with their neighbors and are used to working together more than those living in cities. Because city people lack most of these advantages, food storage is of the utmost importance for their survival.

Some of you will relocate. If this is your emergency plan, then all you need is your 72-hour kit, a place to go and a way to get there. You can drive to almost anywhere in the United States within 72 hours.

We are going to deal with the worst-case scenario. If you are prepared for the worst then anything less will be a walk in the park.

When something bad occurs, most people think everything is going to be all right because the Government will take care of things. **That's not what happened when Katrina hit.** There was no food, and there were riots in the streets.

People who have some food will eat as though nothing is wrong and will use up the six meals worth of food that they have on hand in no time. Some will watch what they eat, and it will last a few days. However, within a week, most people will be out of food. Chaos will ensue, and most people will be forced to leave, hoping to find food somewhere. This is when you, with your food storage, will be safe – that is if you **keep your food storage secret. If not, your neighbors will be at your door and will take your food by any means necessary.**

If you can survive thirty days in the city, you will have the city to yourself. Most people will have left the city with only a few left to run in gangs on the streets. In later chapters we will cover how to deal with the gangs and utilize the remaining resources of the city.

We are going to focus on where and how to store food in the city environment. We will comprise a basic list of food needs. There are many online sites and books with details of how much and what kinds of foods to store. You can find out how long food will keep and how much protein is lost over time. We personally have a CD with 1,200 pages on food storage. This same information as well as this book itself will be on the CD of this book. We will cover the basics here and concentrate on where and how to store your food in the city. The Church of Latter Day Saints has done a great job of providing information to everyone about food storage. You can go to their web site for details or just type in "food storage" online. There are many places where you can buy food ready to store. All of these places have good products. Most importantly, we will cover how and where to store your food.

Below is what one adult man or one adult woman will each need for thirty days or one year, consuming 2,300 calories per day:

	One Year		Thirty Days	
	adult male	adult female	adult male	adult female
Grains	400 lbs	300 lbs	33 lbs	25 lbs
Beans	60 lbs	45 lbs	5 lbs	4 lbs
Cooking oil	10 qts	8 qts	1 qt	.6 qts
Honey	60 lbs	42 lbs	5 lbs	3.5 lbs
Salt	8 lbs	6 lbs	.6 lbs	.5 lbs
Powered milk	16 lbs	12 lbs	1.3 lbs	1 lbs
Drinking water	365 gals	275 gals	30 gals	23 gals

Regarding water, remember that you can go thirty days or more without food, but you will need water right away. A gallon of water weighs 8.3 pounds. That is a great deal of weight to carry around. You will need to plan for that.

Children ages one to three years will need a third of what an adult male requires in food consumption. Children four to six years will require half as much as an adult male. Kids ages seven to nine years will require the same as an adult female. Adults performing manual labor will use a third more calories. This amount of food will keep you and your family alive, but you will not be satisfied.

If you are overwhelmed at this point, don't worry. This book will help you work through the process. It is not as hard as it seems.

There are two thoughts about food storage:

1. I will need my food storage to last for many years, and I will need to store food to last for 10 – 15 or 20 years.
2. I will need my food storage within the next few years and will store a maximum of one year of food.

If you believe it will be a long time before you will need to use your food storage, then you need to go online and get books on long-term food storage. It takes a great deal more money, time and space to store food over a 10 to 20-year period. To store food for 10 years or more, it is best to store it in sealed 5-gallon plastic buckets with Mylar bags and oxygen absorbers. You will need grinders to turn your wheat into flour. This is harder to do for people in the city.

In this book we are not going to deal with the storage of food for 20 years.

This book is to prepare those people who live in big cities and think they will need their food storage within the next few years. It will be easier for city people to work with this type of storage – foods that can be stored and then used and replaced each year. It takes up less space, and less costly equipment is needed to prepare the food for consumption.

You are probably thinking this is too much for me to do, too much money and where will I put it? No it isn't. You can do this! You consume much more than this amount of food in a year right now. You just don't see it all in one place, and you don't buy it all at one time. Think about how many times you go to the store and buy food!

How do you eat an elephant? The answer is one bite at a time. And so it is with food storage. You begin with one can at a time.

Getting started is the hardest part. You will find after you have stored even a small amount of food you will get excited and feel great about yourself and what you are doing. Set a goal to have one week of food stored. You may only want to store one month of food altogether. Whatever your goal, the first thing is to buy that first can.

VERY IMPORTANT DON'TS:

→ Don't tell anyone about your food storage.

→ Don't worry about all the charts out there. They are made up based on what doctors and scientists say are the nutritional needs of a person – not what people really eat.

→ Don't get worried that you have too much of one thing and not enough of another.

→ Don't weigh everything.

→ Don't forget how important your personal preferences are in choosing what foods you store.

→ Don't store foods you don't like even if they are on sale, unless you are going to use them for trading.

→ Don't forget variety. The charts don't deal with this very well. POW's have starved because they only had rice and couldn't stand to eat it anymore.

→ Don't forget to rotate your storage by eating the older food first and replacing it with new.

→ Don't forget to store candy and quick and easy foods for when you are psychological or physically unable to deal with hard jobs.

→ Don't store items with short-term expiration dates. Your stored food needs to last as least a year, or remember to rotate the food at the expiration dates.

Yes, you need a plan, but don't try to be perfect. Anything you accomplish is better than doing nothing and puts you in a better position than you are right now.

First, look at what you have on hand for food right now. How long do you think the food you currently have would last if you couldn't buy any more? That is how much time you would have before you would be in trouble. Then what would you do?

Looking at the food you currently have also tells you what kind of food you like and where to put your money in buying more. It is always best to try to stay with the foods you normally buy and like.

Make a list of the foods that are in cans and sealed bags that don't need refrigeration.

Make a list of things you have, but will not store for a year, such as items in your refrigerator. You will need to find a substitute for those foods if you are going to want them as part of your storage.

Make a list of all the foods you have that will not store, but that you could do without.

Again, remember that you can go a long time without food, but you will need water in just a few days.

Now put together a list of foods you want to store. Then look at the list and see what is missing that you will have to add in some form that you don't currently have. You can find on the web and in books a list of all the foods. In this county, however, we have a large number of people from different backgrounds, religions and races. We could never provide a list of everything for everyone. But, we are going to provide you with guidelines. It is up to you to think specifically about you and you family. How much money do you have for food storage and how much space in which to store it? Only you can decide what is best for you.

Appendix B contains a list of foods for you to review, but you must adjust the list to meet your personal needs. Go to ***www. pipehitterstactical.com*** for helpful details.

Canning:
This is a very important skill to learn. One of the best ways to store real meat is to can it. You can buy whole chickens at a good price, and

the meat will stay good for more than a year. Canning is easy and doesn't cost much. You need a pressure cooker, jars and lids. Everything needed can be found at Wal-Mart along with a book on how to can. You can cube red meats and then can them also. Canning is good for almost everything you need to store, especially fruits and vegetables. The only down side to canning is that the jars are glass and can break.

Starting**:**

After you make your list of needs, it is time to start. Again, don't be overwhelmed. Do what you can, when you can. The worst thing you can do is nothing because you think you can't do it all. Only you know how important this is to you and how much money and time you want to spend on food and water storage.

If you have the funds, then you may want to go online and order all you need. But remember, even if you order a pre-made kit, there are other things that only you use and need. Don't just order a year's supply and think it is everything you need.

The important thing is to start. No matter how small you start, it is a start.

Every time you go to the store for food, buy just one more can of beans and put it aside for storage. **Storing one can at a time will get you there. One can a week is 52 cans of life-saving food at the end of one year!!!!** When there is no food on the store shelves, how much will each can be worth to you?

Make a goal to have a certain number of cans stored each month. Don't forget that everything doesn't have to be good for a year. Remember most people only have enough food for six meals on hand. You will be ahead of everyone if you have more bread, milk and eggs, or items you use each day, than people around you. Even foods that don't store for a year will store well enough for you to have a week of meals on hand all the time, and if you start right away, when something does happen you can make that week's supply last even longer. You will not have to go out into the dangerous streets.

Storing the food**:**

Storage temperature and the length of time food will store is critical. Following is a Department of Defense chart to show you how temperature affects military MRE's (meals ready to eat).

Temperature at storage	Food life
60 degrees F	130 months
70 degrees F	100 months
80 degrees F	76 months
90 degrees F	55 months
100 degrees F	22 months
110 degrees F	5 months
120 degrees F	1 month

→ **Don't** store where it will freeze.
→ **Don't** store in temperatures above 70.
→ **Don't** store in a garage (unless it is heated or has AC).
→ **Don't** store in an attic (unless it is heated or has AC).
→ **Don't** store in a wet environment.

→ **Do** store in a basement (If dry).
→ **Do** store in a crawl space (If dry).
→ **Do** use a magic marker to put a date on everything so you will know when the year is up, or if it has an expiration date, replace it with new food. Eat the oldest food first.
→ **Do** check regularly to make sure none of the cans are dented; dents can cause your food to spoil even if they are not leaking. Open any can that is dented and check it for spoilage. If it's okay, then you can eat it.
→ **Do** check regularly to make sure none of the containers are leaking.

People in the country have more places to store food – basements, crawl spaces, out buildings. In the city you may only have an apartment, but you will be surprised how much you can store in a small apartment. Use your imagination. We will give you some hints, but you are limited only by your imagination and desire to store food.

Most corn, peas, and soup cans are 3 inches wide and 4 inches high. Fruit and some other cans are 4 inches wide and 4 inches high. Be sure to measure the space you have and then the different cans you are thinking about buying to utilize your storage space in the most efficient way.

The kitchen cabinets:
If you look at your kitchen cabinets you will find that more than half the space is not even used. Even if all the shelves are full, there is usually

a good deal of unused space around and above the contents. Stand back with the doors open and you will see there is a great deal of wasted space.

Reorganize your shelves and put all the tall items into one area. Then put cans in one cabinet. You can go to a hardware store and buy extra shelving and add shelves so you can stack more cans in that cabinet.

The broom closet:

If you have a broom closet you will find lots of wasted space there. Try to find a different place to store the items in the broom closet. Hangers can be added on the outside of the closet to hang up the broom and mop. I know it may not look as nice as you would like, but you can't eat a broom or mop. That broom closet full of food might save your life. So, do the same as you did with the kitchen cabinets. Add shelves. Be sure to measure the cans or other foodstuffs you are going to put in that space and make the shelves that height. It is best to put up shelving that is adjustable so you can change the height as needed.

Clothes closets/hall closets/coat closets:

These are places you can store many food cans. This will not interfere with the clothes and will be hidden from view. The closet ends are the best places for storage. Most closets are about 24 inches deep and 96 inches tall. There are two ways to do this. The best way is to buy rails with holes for adjusting the shelves. This is better because you don't have to put the same size cans on each shelf, and you can pick cans from any shelf. It costs more for the shelving and is more work to install. You can hang a cover of some kind over the food so no one can see it. You can measure how wide the wall is at each end of the closet and buy 1 x 4 inch boards, ½ inch shorter than the wall. If you have a hard floor in the closet you can place the cans on the floor to start. If you have a rug then it is best to cut out the first 4 inches of rug. If you don't want to do that then you should start by placing one of the 1 x 4's on the rug first. Then stack cans all the way across the board. Make sure all the cans are the same height. It works well if you use corn or peas in a row. Then add another 1x 4 and stack more cans and repeat. Be aware that it may become unstable it you are stacking on a carpet. You can stack in hall closets and coat closets as well. If you stack soup cans, corn or peas you can stack 144 three-inch cans and 108 four-inch cans in each end of a closet. Look at the back wall of the closet. Depending on the closet depth, you may also be able to put shelves on the back wall.

Most clothes in a closet are items like pants, shirts, coats and other things that don't hang all the way to the floor. This is a good place to store larger cans like those that hold coffee and lard and products that come in cans about the size of a gallon of paint. This is a good place to store your water, as well. Remember, you need two quarts of water per person per day (drinking water). This is a lot of water.

Beds:

Take a good look at each bed. What do the mattresses set on? Here is a place to store lots of food. If there is a frame and the bed is off the floor, then you can put cans under the bed. You can stack cans of the same size on the floor and place a sheet of plywood on them and add another layer of cans and yet another layer of plywood until your bed is as high as you desire.

Furniture:

Look at your furniture and turn it over to see if there is any place for food storage underneath. Footstools are a good place for storage. We made 24-inch by 24-inch footstools with nice padding on them and wheels on the bottom. There is a hinged top to get into the footstool so we can fill them with food. People put their feet on the stools and don't realize there is food stored inside. You can make a nice coffee table and do the same thing, put a hinged top on it and fill it with food.

Look at the space where your furnace and water heater are kept. Is there space for shelves? Make sure you don't put shelves or food in a place that will interfere with the operation of your appliances. However, look at the door to the utility room or where the furnace and water heater are located. You are probably the only one who uses that door, and not that much. You can put shelves on the backside of that door to hold a great deal of food.

Entertainment centers:

Some of you may have an entertainment center with doors on the side of the TV or under the TV area. This is a good pace to store food. Most of us don't keep anything important in that space. Keep the door closed and no one will know. Remember that the time may come when having food is more important then having a place for CDs and DVDs.

Computer tables:
Look over your computer table to see if there is room somewhere inside, on or under it to store food.

Bathroom:
Don't forget the bathroom. The vanity is 20 inches deep. Again, try to put all the things you need for your use in one part of the vanity. You can also add shelves to the vanity to be able to utilize your space better. Just one area in your vanity that is 20 inches deep, 18 inches wide and 30 inches high will hold 120 three-inch cans or 90 four-inch cans.

Guest room/spare room:
If you have a spare room or a guest room, then you have another great place to store your food. If there are closets in those rooms, this is a great place to store the larger items. Some of the foods you buy are sold in multi-packs that take up more room such as coffee and lard and some of the other foods you need to store. And remember, guest or spare rooms are another great space to store water.

Alternative water storage:
If you have some warning of impending disaster, you should fill the tub, sink and all the containers you have that will hold water. Don't forget your water heater. It holds 20 to 100 gallons of water. If you live in an apartment, locate the utility room in your building to find out if you could have access to it and the boiler and/or water heater.

Remember you may not like how some of this storage looks in your home, but if the time comes when you need it, how your home looks will not be important.

For survival foods that are ready to go, contact *www.longlifefoods. com.*

Chapter Four

Personal Choice:
On Your Own or in a Group?

One of the first things you have to decide is if you should try to survive on your own or be with a group. As there are advantages and disadvantages to both, you need to sit down and write a list of the things you have and your plan to survive, and take into consideration if there are more people who you will be responsible for.

If you are going to be on your own, then you will have some advantages over a group. First and foremost, you will not need as much food or water. It will easier for you to hide, and you will be much more mobile. You will be able to run and hide without having to devote time, food or energy to take care of others. You don't have to find large quantities of food or water to survive. It will be harder for people to find you or pursue you if you need to run. However, there are also disadvantages of being on your own. You are more mobile, but if you have to move you will have to carry all your supplies by yourself. If you become sick or are injured, you will have to take care of yourself. You cannot perform CPR on yourself. Also, consider whether you really want to survive if you are all alone.

If you are going to be a part of a group then there are many things you need to consider. First, how many people should you have in your group, and how many can you support with the supplies you have? Any people you are going to include in your group should also participate in your plan and be storing food, water and supplies, as well.

One advantage of a group is that you have more people to share the workload, and there are more skill sets available. There may be both males and females in the group. Companionship is important. You should sit down and make a list of the skills you will need to survive and then make up a list of people who have the skills you need. Remember, you will be doing things that most of you have never had to do. When you trap an animal, who in your group knows how to skin and prepare it for cooking? Who knows how to trap and hunt? You will need people to repair your vehicles, chain saws or other tools you will be using. You can no longer take your chain saw blade to the store to have it sharpened.

It will not be easy to pick which individuals to admit into your group. You will want to use your heart to choose, but remember that every person in your group needs to be able to contribute as much to the group as they take. It is going to be hard; the old and sick are the people we wish to take care of, but they will only use food and water that may be better used on others who contribute to the group. This is hard to consider, but necessary.

You are going to have to make hard decisions. With limited food and water and medical supplies, you are not going to be able to save everyone you want. It is important to talk through and think about all these choices you may have to make before the hard times come. It is going to be hard to make those decisions, but it is going to be even harder when you are low on food and you are not thinking clearly. Also, when the time comes, there will be many people who have no skills and didn't listen to your warning, so they don't have any food or water. They will be putting pressure on you to join your group. You really need to make more of these decisions before the time comes then to have to make this kind of choice in a time of emergency.

Most people around you will not be prepared and will do anything to survive, so again, it is important that you keep your food storage a secret. People will come to you for food and water and your first instinct will be to give it to them. It will make you feel good that you could help. But remember to ask yourself, if you give them food and water whose food and water do you give them? Do they receive the food and water and medicines that you have for your family; are you going to let your children die because you gave someone who did nothing to be prepared, your children's food and water? You cannot have too much food and water stored!

Some people may not possess any skill that you can see, but they may be important. If you are religious you may want a clergyman, and that may be the only thing he or she contributes to the group. But this may be very important to the emotional stability and motivation of the group. It is at these times, that college degrees and money will have very little value. Everyone needs to learn skills that will be of benefit in a survival environment. There will be little need for attorneys. Skills that are very important and worth a great deal of money now, may be of little value in a survival group.

Before a time of emergency comes, you should think about what kind of an organization you are going to use for a group. You may need a different organization at first than you will need later on. At first you may only need or want a single person in charge. When the disaster hits, people will be looking for leadership, someone to take charge and get things done. It is important to get things done quickly, and it will help keep people calm if they see there is a plan and someone in charge. Later however, after things have calmed down, you may want to set up a committee to govern or have different people in charge of different things. This will keep people calm if they have something to do and are not just sitting around worrying. It is also important for people to see that they have some control over their lives. There will be more cooperation if people have a job to do and a need to get up and do something. They need to feel a part of the group and realize that there is hope and a reason to keep going.

It would be wise to watch some movies or TV series such as: ***Jericho, The Colony, The Road, The Book of Eli*** and ***The Day After,*** a nuclear disaster, (1983), ***The Day after Tomorrow***, a 2004 movie about a natural disaster. These are just shows, but they will give you some idea of how people will act following a disaster. Please remember that the main thing missing in these shows is that they never show how violent it is going to get. You will not see some of the violent things that you are going to have to do to survive.

You will have people in your group who will steal from the group or will refuse to do their share of the work. This is going to cause you problems; you need to think about what you would do about this kind of situation now while you are in the planning stage. Most people are not prepared for the violence that is coming their way. It's important to think about who will decide what to do with people who steal. Do you lock them up? Then what, they just sit there and eat your food and water while everyone else has to work for their food? You really need to think about this right now, not when the time actually comes.

You need to make rules for the group and print them out so that those you are considering allowing into the group read them, sign them and agree to live by those rules.

This is going to be hard, but what about people from outside your group who want to join your group? Who again will decide if they can join or not, and if you say "no" what will you be willing to do to survive with your group and keep others from taking or using your life-sustaining supplies?

In this book we are not going to discuss the use of weapons for self defense and offensive tactics. We are talking about your group and its rules. We will talk about how to hide, but not how to fight. Coming out right after this book will be ***"Surviving A Hostile City II"*** in which we will cover offensives and defensive tactics and how to deal with the violence out in the streets and around you.

Chapter Five

Should I Leave the City?

No! You will be better off if you have your food storage so you can stay where you are.

The only time it is better to leave is if you have made arrangements in advance and have a place to go that has shelter, food, water and fuel, or if your area is made unfit to live in by the disaster. You will also need to have good transportation to get there. If you are going to leave, leave as soon as you can before everyone else tries to leave and ties up the roads. If you have not made arrangements, you will not have much of a chance to survive.

Remember in the chapter about food storage where it shows how much food it takes for each person to survive for a year? That means you will have to have all that food put in place somewhere and then keep rotating it or you will have to take it all with you. You would need a big truck for all that.

There are very important things to consider before you decide to leave:

Where will you go?
Everywhere you go people will be in the same situation you are and will be trying to survive too. There is not going to be a place waiting for you and people with open arms to help. You most likely will not have the skill set needed to live off the land. There is not much to live off if you are in a desert area, for example, and you would need skills and equipment that you don't have. You can't eat grass, and most of the crops are meant for animals, not people, and would only be available at harvest time. You will encounter people who will be hostile and may harm you and your family. They may take what you have. Most small towns will be more organized and will not allow anyone into their town to take their supplies. People who live in small towns will have weapons and not hesitate to use them. The police in small towns will not be friendly to outsiders. No one

21

will want to feed more people, let alone outsiders from the city. Think it over before you leave, where will you go?

How will you get there?

You will need good transportation and fuel. Think about what might happen if your car breaks down. How much fuel will you need? You can't count on finding parts or fuel on the way. In fact, if you are stopped, someone may take what you have as well as your car and your fuel.

How will you live on the way?

Don't forget water weighs 8.3 pounds per gallon. You will need food for the trip. If anyone is on medication, you will need that. Where will you get the next supply? You can't count on anyone else to help you along the way. You will not have enough to share with others, and others will not share with you.

How can we live when we get there?

Unlike what most people think, just because you see animals and crops out in the country, that doesn't mean you can survive there. You can't eat grass like the cows; they have four stomachs and use a great deal of water. It takes time to plant and grow food; how will you live until you can harvest it? Do you have seeds and equipment to plant and till the ground? Do you have the equipment to prepare the food you grow and a way to cook it? It is too hot in the desert, and what if it is January and only 10 degrees with snow in the North? You will need shelter and food and water. Don't forget you will need medical supplies and knowledge of what to do if you or your loved ones become sick or get hurt.

Even if you grow your own food, what will prevent others from taking it from you?

Chapter Six

Staying in place and

Scavenging for food – fuel – water and supplies

Attention: Remember trespassing, breaking and entering, and stealing are illegal! Even if there is a crisis and the city is abandoned, and there is no functioning government, laws will not be suspended. We are not telling you to commit crimes or break the law. We are pointing out ways to obtain food and supplies in a crisis. It is up to you to decide to what extent you are willing to go to obtain food and supplies. Remember, trespassing, breaking and entering and stealing is illegal!

Scavenging is another name for looting. When you are out scavenging for food and water and others come by your place and take your supplies, you will think of them as looters for doing the same thing you are doing. You will not have to resort to high-risk operations to survive if you have enough food storage on hand.

Before you go out, think about how badly you want to do this – are you willing to take a life for food, and are you willing to die trying to get it? Others out there will be!

Within five days from when the crisis occurs, the streets will be full of people hunting for food or looters stealing everything, mostly things they don't need. This is not the time to go into the streets. Stay where you are and live off your food storage until everyone leaves the city.

In Los Angeles and New Orleans films showed people looting and taking things they didn't need to survive, like large TV's. There was no power to run the TV's, but the looters would have taken your life in an instance for a TV that they couldn't use. You will find that after 30 days most people are gone, and there are many things you can use still available to you out there. The looters were all about greed and money.

But, remember, you can't eat a TV or cook food with a microwave when there is no power.

Scavenging is a high-risk operation and most of the time will reward you with very little. During the first few days, people will be out trying to find food and supplies. Within a few days there will be no food or water to buy or steal. After three or four days and the people see that no one is going to come and help them, they will start to panic. How long this will take depends on communications. If radio and TV are down and people don't know what is going on, then they will panic very quickly. Personally, as we saw after a hurricane, people soon took everything in a Wal-mart, not just food and water, but everything, and that was within four days after the hurricane. Soon everything will be gone, the people will have taken things they don't need, hoping to sell them later or have them when the power comes back on.

The longer you can stay off the streets the better off you are. At first there will be looting. Then many will try to leave the city. This is going to be hard, because the streets will be full of cars and people all trying to leave not knowing where they are going, just realizing that they can't stay in the city. If you go into the streets at this point, everyone will be trying to take what you have. After a week or so, most of the people will be out of supplies and will have left the city or be in shelters if there are any.

Some people will not leave because they think staying there and waiting for help is best. Some will not have a way to leave, and some will just not want to leave their homes. In a short time the only people left in the city will be without food and water and desperate to find it. They will tend to run in gangs, going from building to building or house to house looking for anything they can use. Some will be gangs like you normally think of, but most will be ordinary people who live around you and are now out of food and water. Make no mistake these people will be more dangerous than the regular street gangs. Desperate people will do desperate things to survive. They will leave, or kill each other, or you. Again, this is the worst time for you to be on the streets. **This is another reason having food storage is so important.**

Many of the apartments or homes around you are now yours to use and search for supplies. This is when knowing how to pick a lock is useful. There is much information on the web on how to pick locks, and you can buy a pick set. But I will tell you that you will not do well without some hands-on training. We have picked locks all over the world, and it has often saved our lives. If you can go to a school, again, it would be of great benefit for you to go to an urban survival school. It will teach you lock picking and many other skills. *www.pipehitterstactical.com* gives urban survival training in locations all over the United States that includes lock picking.

Places to Search for Food and Supplies ~
→ **Wal-mart, Home Depot and other big box stores:**
    The looters will have taken most of the food and water from the most obvious places like Wal-mart and grocery stores. Remember, they will take things they don't need like TV's, even when there is no power. They think they can just sit and wait, and someone is going to come and help them and feed them. That is not very likely to happen.
    You can still go to Wal-mart and find things you can use. You should have a camp stove to cook, and there will be fuel for that stove because no one will have taken it since most don't have a camp stove. You will find wire and duct tape and things you can use. There will be fishing equipment; just look around for the things you should already have but could use more of. All the stores will have a break room for the employees, so there should be food that was kept there in the back of the store for the employees. Look in the back for the forklifts; many may run off LP gas, so you can use the LP gas tanks for heat and cooking. Don't forget to look for animal food – some would be good enough for you to eat, or you can use it to feed the animals you are raising for food or for bait to trap animals.

→ **Sporting good stores:**
    The people will have taken the guns and ammo. Hopefully, you won't need that because you already have your weapons and ammo. Again, you will be after things the looters didn't need or take such as camping and cooking fuels. Maybe they will have missed the dehydrated foods in the camping area. Make a list of things you need to hunt and trap and to use in making traps. These are the things you will be looking for and the things looters most likely will have left. Also, look for containers that can hold water.

→ **Hotels:**
    Most hotels and motels serve at least a breakfast, so somewhere there may be food hidden. These places are also a good source of water. They have large water heaters that can accommodate large numbers of people and many baths at one time. Most of the water in a water heater is good to drink. Remember to boil it or add chemicals if you have any doubt about the water before you drink it. If there is a pool or hot tub, that water is good to use to wash yourself and your cloths, and it is good

to use to flush your toilet. There should be a good supply of pillows and blankets. Again, make a list of things you need, and search for them.

→ **Book Stores:**

These are not places where most looters will go. But most bookstores today sell soft drinks, chips, coffee, bottled water and snack foods. Or you may need to fix some equipment or create something you need, and after looking for food you can search the "how to" books section.

→ **Schools:**

Schools serve lunches and have bottled water. They also have large water heaters. Look in teachers' desks; you may find candy bars and snacks. Check the students' lockers for food and water. School buses are transportation and may have fuel in their tanks.

→ **Self-storage unit:**

When a crisis hits, most people will not have had the time or ability to take all the stuff they had out of their storage units. We went through storage units once overseas in a war zone, and we could have filled a truck with the food, weapons, water and supplies we found.

→ **Gas stations:**

People will have taken the fuel to flee town and any food and water they see, however, look for food, water and soft drinks in the back of the gas station buildings or above the rooms in the attic areas. If there is no electricity, then no one could get to the gas in the underground tanks. Remember to look at all the places we have talked about to see if there are generators that were for sale or for the owners' use in case of an emergency. If you can find a generator, you can pump the gas or use it for lighting or heat.

→ **Non-food business:**

Look for businesses that sell clothing or shoes, or any places where you would not normally think there would be food. Most of these businesses have a break room for the employees, and you might find food and water there. The computer repair shop will have a break room. As you walk around, look at the businesses and think about the break rooms.

→ **Factories:**

Factories and large industrial buildings are another important place to search. If they had many employees then they had restrooms and break rooms. These may also have water storage units inside. They may have different types of fuel stored there. They will most likely have animals running around to hunt and trap. Watch where the animals are going to feed – they may lead you to a supply of food.

→ TV & Radio stations:

Most TV and radio stations are set up to stay on the air during emergencies for long periods of time and should have food and water stored there. They will also have some type of generator for power and fuel to power the generator.

→ ZOO:

If you have a zoo, you have a good source for protein. Remember, it takes lots of food to feed all the animals in a zoo. They should have food and water stored all around, and almost every animal in the zoo can be eaten.

→ Auto parts stores:

This is a good place to find batteries for cars and small batteries. These are good for running lights and pumps. This store will have tools, clamps and tape. These are all things you will need, and not as many people will be looting a store like this. If people do loot here they will be taking other things. Remember, there are few liquids for drinking, but anti-freeze and windshield washer are good for cleaning and flushing the stool. Remember to make a list of things you are looking for and take it with you. Look around; your may find things you don't expect to find in a store like this.

→ Farm supply stores:

These stores are good for many things, animal food, rope, animal traps or things to make traps. There will be tools, and most of these stores will have medicines for animals. Later we will tell you how to use animal medicines to treat humans.

Medicines:

Remember, more people will die from infections and lack of medicines than from lack of food and water or from bullets. You should always be looking for medicines and medical supplies everywhere you go. Hopefully, you will have a good supply in your food storage, and you will not have to risk your life going out into the unsafe streets in search of medicines.

The mobs will have raided all the pharmacies and Wal-marts and anywhere there are medicines. Many people can't read the labels and won't know what they are looking for. Many of them will be looking for narcotics and painkillers. But, they will take everything and then throw away everything they can't use, or trade it for food and water.

Look in abandoned vehicles, in all buildings and in employee lockers. In homes, look in the bathrooms or anywhere you might put your medicines. You should have a **PDR (physician desk reference)** in your storage. If not, then you will have to scavenge for one. This will give you a picture of every medicine out there and how to use it. Remember that schools have a nurse and medications. Fire stations and sports stadiums or anywhere people come to play sports will have types of medications and medical supplies. Veterinarians will have a great deal of medications that you can use for humans. Gas stations and truck stops will have some types of over-the-counter medications and supplies.

Water:

Waterbeds hold lots of water that you can use if you find one in a house, and other people may not have thought of this. Water heaters are in homes and businesses and factories. Swimming pools will have water. Public pools may have water, but most of the people who are not prepared will only be able to dip out water in pails or buckets and it will be hard to carry. You can use a wagon or a shopping cart that you have fitted with some kind of a water bladder, and with a small pump you should have found or had in your storage, you can use a battery or battery-powered drill to run the pump.

Look in basements of apartment buildings. When it comes to water, you may have to drink water that you would never have thought about drinking before. It may look dirty, and it may be, but filter it with you shirt, then boil it and add bleach. It may not smell or look good, but it may save your life.

A good source of water is the water that runs off the roofs of buildings. When you are out scavenging for food remember to keep an eye open for containers that will hold water and hoses or pipes or tubs to collect water. Fire trucks have water! Storm drains have water. All the water that falls on a city will end up in the storm drains and then move out of the city. Remove the lids and see where it is going – some drains are big enough to walk through. All the water that runs off the streets and the roofs of the building has to go somewhere.

Remember to treat all the water from run off; it will have come in contact with many materials, and some may be toxic.

Chapter Seven

Medical

Next to food storage, this is the most important chapter in the book. During times of disasters more people died of infection, lack of medicine or lack of medical treatment than starvation. This is not a first aid book or medical "how to" book. We are going to point out how things may be and what you will need to know, and have, in the way of medical knowledge and supplies. It would take a hundred books to teach you how to do all you need to know about medical skills. It is going to be up to you to decide how much training and supplies you need. You may want to have someone in your group who is a doctor or medic, or you may want to take some kind of medical training. You should definitely have a good first aid book and a PDR (physician desk reference) to provide you with some information about medicines and medical supplies.

Before we talk about all the things you cannot fix, need training for, or need a great deal of medicines to cure, we will cover some of the positive aspects about humans. Humans seem to have a great ability for their bodies to fight back and to survive. A hundred years ago people didn't run to the doctor for every little problem, and they often healed without a problem. Even now the records show that over 80% of people who go to the doctor – not the ER or hospital – but their family doctor, would get well on their own without any medicines or help from the doctor. It may take longer to get over whatever you have, and you may be more uncomfortable until you do, but in the end you would recover, with or without the doctor.

Ninety percent of all the medical problems you are going to deal with can be handled with a first aid book and a well-equipped first aid kit. Most of you will survive. We are going to discuss some of the things that you may have to deal with that are going to be hard to handle from which many people are going to die. Don't become overwhelmed with what we are going to discuss. It is bad, and some of this may happen to you, but don't give up on obtaining some training and storing medical supplies, because you can't save everyone from everything. You will not be able to deal with some of the worst things, but those type of problems are going to be a small part of your medical needs.

When you read the information below, remember that this is a small part of what is going to happen. Again, don't become overwhelmed and give up. What is listed below will be less than 5% of what you will be dealing with. Obtain CPR training and take a Red Cross first aid course. Collect a great deal of basic medical supplies, such as a large first aid kit and you will be able to take care of 90% of your medical needs and problems.

In Vietnam and other war zones and disaster areas around the world, most of the people we helped and lives we saved were due to our basic first aid skills and the supplies we carried. As in Vietnam and other places, sanitation was a big factor in the health of the people. There will be no running water to wash with after you use the bathroom during disaster times, so have alcohol available to clean you hands. This will help to stop the spread of disease more easily than treating people after they have gotten sick.

To treat the health problems and perform the procedures listed below, you can take EMT training. We also give a three-day course on how to deal with the kind of medical problems listed below, and it is geared for the average person to take and understand, *(pipehitterstactical. com)*.

You need to have the mindset that it is July 1863 at the Battle of Gettysburg, and you are the doctor. There is no one coming if you call 911 and no place to go to get help. What are you going to do? In fact, a 2010 committee report stated that U.S. hospitals received an "F" when it came to being prepared for a bio-terrorist attack. In addition, a survey showed that even the most dedicated hospital staffers will abandon their posts when confronted with a bio-terrorist emergency at their hospitals.

First, you must realize that you are not going to be able to save everyone, and some will not be worth using up you medicines to save. You may have to let some die to save others. Preparing your mind to make those decisions is going to be harder than most of the things you need to do to prepare for a disaster.

Look at all the medicines you, your family or people in your group are using now. You need to list them and see which ones you actually need to keep people alive day by day. If you have people who have to take a medicine every day to stay alive, and they only have a 30-day supply, then they are going to die when their medicine runs out. People who need to have treatments to stay alive such as chemo and dialysis will also die. You may have a person in your family or group who has an ostomy bag or who needs catheters. People on heart medications and insulin will not have much of a chance to survive. You should try to keep as much of the life-saving medicines on hand as you can. After a disaster hits, you may also be able to scavenge and find additional maintenance medications. The looters will have taken all the pain medications, but they may not want or need the maintenance types of medicines. Or, perhaps they will take everything they see because they don't know which ones to take. You may be able to trade for some of these later. (We will talk about storing items for trading in a later chapter.)

You cannot wait until you need medicines to obtain them. You can talk to your physician and explain your concerns. He may give you a 60 or 90 day supply. You can try going to Canada or Mexico to buy the medicines you need in larger amounts. Your insurance company may not pay for more than a 30 day supply, so ask if you can buy more and pay for it yourself.

There are so many bad things that can happen, and accidents will be more prevalent. You will be doing work that you may not normally do, and you will be out of shape for doing all the physical things you are now going to be doing. You will have a better chance of hurting your back and doing damage to your muscles, and you will certainly be more tired than you are now. Unfortunately, at the same time you will have less food to eat. Your general health is going to go down from what it is now. You will be working harder and longer and performing heavier work with less food and water. You will be making more mistakes, and that will lead to more accidents. You will need a great deal of aspirins and ace bandages.

We are going to point out below some of the things that can happen. These may not be a big part of your problems, but you need to consider them.

Triage: Please understand that you will need to use a different method to determine who should be treated first and for whom you will use your precious medicines. Right now we are used to treating the person who is in the worst condition first. When you come upon an accident, you look everyone over, and the ones who are not hurt too badly you leave and instead treat the ones who may die first. You will have to start thinking like the military thinks. The person who will take little supplies and time should come first. With a little help, they can survive and possibly get back to helping you. When you are in combat you look everyone over, and the person with the head wound that may not make it is treated last, not first. Just as on the battlefield, you are going to be limited on medical supplies, and you won't be able to waste them on people who are not going to survive anyway. This is going to be one of the hardest things you will have to do, but remember although it may feel good to save someone, you may be endangering the life of someone else who needs the medicine and would survive.

Broken bones: There are many kinds of breaks, but you need to think only about two kinds, simple fracture (the bone doesn't come out of the skin) and compound fracture (the bone comes out of the skin). Unless you have a doctor or someone who is skilled in setting bones, the only thing you can do is splint the break and let it heal as it is. In the early days when a farmer broke his leg this is all people did, so the farmer walked with a limp the rest of his life. In those days, if a person was lucky, they had a local doctor who would try to set the break – that is to pull it and move it back into place. This really didn't work most of the time; sometimes it did more damage than good. Moving the broken bone can cut muscle or a vein, and the person can bleed to death. Doctors today take x-rays to view the break before attempting to set it. Regarding compound breaks, during a time of catastrophe if you have an accident and the bone comes out of the skin, you will have to do what the doctors at Gettysburg did and cut off the limb. Today on any normal day, it would take a hospital and a team of doctors, an Orthopedic Surgeon, a Neurologist, and Anesthesiologist along with the OR staff to repair a compound break.

There are going to be many people getting cut, so you will need to have a suture kit and learn how to sew lacerations. This is not hard to learn to do and will be of great value to you.

Infections will kill many people, so you need to have a good stock of products that will kill germs. You can use alcohol or bleach. You should stock many items such as Neosporin. Try to find and keep any antibiotics you have around. You can go to places that sell farm supplies and find antibiotics. We have talked to veterinarians, and they tell us that the antibiotics they use on animals are of the same quality as for humans. The difference is in how much you use. The label is made to instruct you on how much antibiotic to use on a horse or cow. However, if you read the label and refer to your medical manual or PDR, it will tell you how much to give a human. Then you need to convert the amount for the animal to what you need for humans. At the farm supply store you will find needles, syringes, IV bags and the supplies you will need to give IV's.

You should have a great deal of aspirin on hand; it is good for pain as well as fever, however, aspirin thins the blood, so you need Tylenol, too. It helps with pain and fever but does not thin the blood. If you have someone on blood thinners for their heart you won't want to give them aspirin. I can't stress enough how important it is going to be to have good medical books and to have some medical training.

<u>Biological</u>:

No matter if there is a natural catastrophe or a terrorist attack, the best defense is a good offense. Go get your vaccinations for yellow fever, Anthrax, hepatitis A and B, typhoid, and your flu shot every year. If you become infected, it will be too late. You would have a hard time surviving even if you could go to a hospital; prevention is the answer to surviving biological agents.

<u>Chemical</u>:

Most of the time if you are exposed to agents such as nerve gases and other deadly gases, there is little you can do for yourself. The medicine the military uses is a controlled product and very hard to obtain. Stay inside. You need to keep eyewashes and items nearby to clean your skin if you are exposed. There is not much else you can do. Cleaning the eyes and skin with clean water can treat non-lethal agents such as tear gas and pepper spray. Unfortunately, clean water will be hard to come by; you should have bottles of sterile water in your storage.

<u>Gunshot wounds</u>:

Most people die from gunshot wounds due to blood loss. A bullet can also break bones and puncture lungs. If the wound is fatal, most people die within a few minutes or bleed to death in a short time. The best things you can do is administer first aid, stop the bleeding and make sure the airway is clear; treat for shock. For loss of blood, for shock and many other issues, it is good to have IV's on hand and learn how to give them. It is not as hard as you think and doesn't take too much training – you are not going to apply to work at a hospital. Again there are many places where you can learn how to set up and give an IV. We will show you how in our off the grid medical class. You can sign up for this class at ***www.pipehitterstactical.com.***

Surviving a Hostile City IV will be dedicated entirely to survival medicine.

33

Chapter Eight

Hiding in Plain Sight

Camouflage & Hardening your Shelter

The first 30 days following a disaster will be the most dangerous time to be on the streets. If you have at least a 30-day supply of food and water, you will be able to ride out the hardest times and not have to leave your home or apartment to go into the streets.

Remember burglars ride around and look for homes with four or five newspapers lying on the front porch and no lights on in the house. That tells them that no one is there, that maybe the owners were on vacation, and this would be a good home to break into. Well, you need to think this way in reverse. People will have left the city, and gangs will be running the streets looking for food or anything they can get their hands on. People and gangs will be going from house-to-house and building-to-building ransacking them. You want them to pass you by.

Camouflage (Hiding in plain sight):

You want your shelter to look like no one is there and that others have already been there looting. You have seen on TV the mess that is left behind after people loot – that is how you want your place to appear. You need to throw things in the lawn and on the porch and in the hallway. Make it hard for people to get to your door, put things in the way. Just don't be neat, don't make it look as though you placed things there. Make it appear as though junk was thrown there. Make it so they have to step over things to get in and out. **Don't make a path.** Do this to every home or apartment near you, on both sides for four or five places. Break out windows and have things hanging out the windows of the homes around you. There will be many places that have not been looted, so most likely people will not waste time looking in places that appear like they have already been looted.

Vehicles – if you have a car or truck, it is not good to put it in a garage. If people see that a garage door is not open, they will break in to see what is inside looking for fuel. You should leave your garage door open and have the doors of the car or truck open with stuff piled on it and in it so that it looks like it has be looted also. We have taken a few wires and taped them under the dash with a lot of wires hanging out under the dash making it look like someone has tried to jump the wiring to start the car. Leave a hose hanging out of the gas tank to look as though someone has already taken your gas.

Have sanitary containers marked "poison" or "hazardous material" in which to hide food, water or supplies.

It is easier and safer to hide than to fight.

Most people are lazy. If they see homes down the road that are easy to get to, they will not mess with yours. They won't waste time on yours if they think someone else has already been there.

You should use a room or two in the back of your home or apartment to live in. Pick rooms with small windows that are hard to see into from the outside. Throw furniture and clothing in the room where the main entrance is so if people do come up to the door and look in, it will look like the outside, as if it has been looted too. You will want to lock the front door, but don't. If someone comes up to it, and it is locked, they will think there is something worth locking them out for and will break in to look around the rest of the house.

Think about when you drove around town, you could tell when a home had been abandoned. This is the same thing; people will be looking for homes that are not abandoned. This will be a hard way to live, but your life may depend on it. Even if you have weapons, there may be too many people to fight. We will talk later about where, when and how to fight and win.

It would be best to spread all your supplies around, using other buildings so if someone does get to you and your supplies, you won't lose everything. *Surviving A Hostile City II* will teach you how to defend yourself and fight back.

Hardening your Shelter:
You need to make the room or rooms in which you are going to live safe from gangs. Live in a back room, cover the windows with plywood or something solid, and screw it in place. Put dead bolts and cross bracing bars on the door. You need to make this room so that you can go in there and defend yourself and your loved ones. This is the hard part. You will have to make a plan and think about it. Even with weapons, you can

only fight so many people at one time. There may come a time when it is better to move out and hide. You should make places in other buildings around you that you could run to and hide. That is another reason why you should have supplies in other buildings. You should pick places that will provide you with both concealment (can't see you) and cover (will stop a bullet).

You will have to think about your choices. Hide in the safe room. Fight from the safe room or run. Remember if there are a lot of people, they may just wait outside and burn your house down. So you need to think about how to get away if you need to.

In *Surviving A Hostile City II*, we will talk about the best way to deal with large numbers of people and which weapons to use.

Chapter Nine

Gangs

Street Gangs:

When most people think of gangs, they think of street gangs. These are groups that wear something to show they are in a gang, motorcycle gang, or street gangs of all kinds. We have talked to many people and watched movies or TV shows about disasters and chaos in the streets, and it seems that everyone has the same ideas about how the gangs are going to fit into the picture. They see them as tough and mean, killers and organized groups with lots of guns. Shows depict them as running and ruling the streets, and most show them taking over the food warehouses and killing everyone for food.

Let's talk about the food warehouses in big cities. We have looked at what most people think of as food warehouses. Most people think of these as huge buildings with enough food to stock or re-supply many supermarkets. There are no magic buildings like this anywhere. There are a few buildings with paper goods and maybe some canned food, but the bread is baked in a local or regional plant and shipped daily to the markets. This is the same with milk and frozen foods. It costs too much to have large buildings with freezers to store frozen foods; most come right from the manufacturer in refrigerated trucks to the market. There are no large buildings with fresh fruit, watermelon, tomatoes, and produce. This type of food comes in from farms or local pickers, or all the way from Texas. However, there are no magic buildings in cities in which you will find food, and neither will the gangs.

In most cities, all the food that is stored is enough to last for about seventy-two hours. What buildings there are that may have some value are on a list at homeland security, and those buildings will be the first ones to be taken over by the authorities. Do you know where the trucks that you see coming to your local market are coming from? No? Well, neither do the gangs.

In considering the gangs, it's true they are hard and will kill without hesitate. But they are not well organized except maybe for selling drugs.

They don't get along well with each other; they only see the gang as an organization to help them as an individual. Their strength is as a group, and on their own they are nothing. They may be mean, but that will not stop bullets. Most gang members are in poor health, overweight, drink too much, use drugs, and smoke. This means they can't move fast and can't run, because they can't breath well. Most have some kind of health problem like sugar and lung issues. You don't see gang members going to the gym or working out. Because they can't move fast, they will make good targets. Make no mistake, in a group and on their ground, they will kill you, but you have so much going for you that you need not be afraid of them. You need to get over your fear and use your brain. Gang members usually have lots of ink on their arms, but tattoos will not make them strong and bullet proof.

When it comes to guns, gangs have many handguns, because they can carry them without being seen. I am sure they have AK-47s, shotguns and weapons like that hidden somewhere. I have never seen gangs training with these types of weapons – going out and shooting your beer can after it's empty is not training. I am sure there are gang members who have been in the military or had some training, but they don't keep their training up. Gangs will be a problem in the first few days. When things are bad on the streets, gangs will be looting and taking all they can. But like at Katrina, people were stealing TV's and appliances, and so will the gangs. You can't eat a TV. Gang members will be likely to pick on small groups of people who are unarmed and who they out number. This is another reason you need your food storage so that you don't have to go out into the dangerous streets at first. Even if you have weapons, it will not help in finding food. Where will you go to steal it? In a few days the whole city will be out of food. Gang members may be mean, but just like you they will need food and water. In five to seven days, they will be in big trouble, maybe more than the average person because they are in poor health. Also, all the good people in the city will have no hesitation shooting a gang member. I think most people would shoot them now if it were not against the law. So shooting gang members in a time of disaster will be easy for people, and the police will think of it as a duty to shoot the gang members.

After ten days to two weeks, during a major disaster, everyone is going to realize there is no food and no help coming. They are going to leave the cities. This is the same with the gangs; they will soon realize there is nothing in the cities for them, and they will leave and head for the country and small towns. In the books we've read, the movies we have seen and the TV shows we watch, everything shows the gangs going to small towns and taking them over killing the people, raping and stealing the food. The books, movies, and shows all seem to depict the small town people as nice, religious, family-orientated people who will be helpless. While it may be true that small town people are family- orientated people who are nice and religious, don't mistake kindness for weakness.

The small town where I grew up in Indiana is just like that. Everyone knows each other and helps each other. If you would come to that town right now and your car broke down, people would help you. You would think they are great people, and they are. But when disaster hits and a gang comes to their town, it would be like running a gauntlet of bullets. The nice townspeople don't like gangs now, and if you think they are going to let big city gangs have their food and kill their families, you are wrong. The gangs will go to the small towns, and that will be the end of the gangs.

Chapter Ten

Gardening
by *Ron Kauffman*

Gardening is a way to feed yourself and family. You can add variety to your diet and become healthier. Now, lets be honest with ourselves, there is work involved in a successful garden. You will get out of it what you put into it. If you are one of those who think that if green stuff was fit to eat, God would not have given you teeth, then you are a carnivore. Don't waste your time reading this chapter. Refer to the chapters on Zebra steaks and other zoo delights. Or review the chapter on a cannibal's easy pickings, homeless stew and other recipes.

Gardening is not a quick fix. It takes work and time to reap the rewards of a garden. None of this will happen overnight. Most plants take 60 to 90 days to produce a harvestable crop. Some crops like potatoes, tomatoes, squash, and most root crops require more time. Many of the salad crops, lettuce, spinach and other greens can start producing in 60 days and continue until a frost kills them. No matter where you live, there is a limited growing season. That season determines what you can grow outside. You can extend the growing period by providing a protective covering from the elements. I live in northeastern Indiana and can enjoy fresh lettuce all year long by planting a crop in September or early October. I do so in a cold frame made of 2X8's with a glass patio door on top and soil scooped around the outside. I walked outside on New Year's Day and shoveled a foot of snow off the glass. That was so I could enjoy a great salad for dinner. It was a great way to start a new year.

Plants are wondrous things; all they need is soil, water, sunlight and a few warm days. A garden need not be a large space in the open. It can be as small as a few pots on a windowsill, a large planter on a patio or bag of soil split open on the back porch. You can even hang a plastic bag of soil from a rafter and watch tomatoes grow upside down.

This particular book is for city dwellers. You may not have a backyard you can use as a garden space. There may not be a vacant lot that can become a community garden. Two legged rodents may be a real problem. You may have to become very creative and do your gardening in pots. The requirements are still the same – soil, water, sunlight and, oh yes, seeds. I keep saying sunlight; there are special grow lights for indoor plants that you could use. If things have really gone down the tubes, you may not have electricity or running water. If that is the case, I hope you have seeds stored for your garden. Let's talk about seeds. There are two types – hybridized and natural or non-hybrid. Natural seed are unchanged and will reproduce themselves. Hybridized are altered seeds and will produce only one crop. Tomatoes are a good example. The ones you buy in the store are bred for color, storage life and eye appeal. You'll notice I did not include taste, three out of four, that's not too bad. When you buy seeds, look for the natural seeds. These are sometimes labeled Heritage seeds. They are the old varieties that have been passed down unchanged. Many seeds come from plants that have been crossed to bring out the best in them genetically. They have not gone so far that the seeds are sterile. The last of the crop can be allowed to go "to seed" and saved until next year. Seeds can be saved for four or five years if stored properly in a cool dry place. There are many sources of seeds. A local garden center is a good place to start. You may see seeds in a grocery store or a hardware center. There are many mail-order houses that have seeds. Their catalogs are fun to look at and offer many useful hints. Buy a good quality of seed. Cheap seeds at a discount store are just that. Their quantity is less and their age may be unknown. They may be a good buy or not. Keep in mind that seeds are not available all year long. You should buy extra and store them for next year. An airtight jar in the back of the refrigerator would be a safe place. It is not necessary to plant a whole packet of seeds at once. Space the planting out a couple of weeks apart. That way you have fresh vegetables all summer long. If you are canning or trading for something else, you may need a large crop at one time. It is possible to get three or four plantings a season. Some seeds are very small and it is not possible to spread them out. These are sowed and not planted a seed at a time. What you MUST do is thin them out as they come up so each plant can develop to full size. Lettuce and carrots are good examples. You don't have to let plants mature before you start eating them. Baby carrots and new lettuce are very good.   You have many choices of what to plant: peas, radishes, onions, spinach, cabbage, Swiss chard, beets, carrots, lettuce, beans, corn, cucumbers, zucchini, squash, peppers and tomatoes. These are just some of your choices. There are many varieties of each.

Don't let them become confusing. It is important to think about what you will grow in terms of what you will eat. It is a waste of time and effort to grow something you don't like and may not eat, unless you can trade it for something else. One of the most common mistakes people make is thinking too big. Keep it small and simple, something you can spend a few minutes each day and enjoy doing. To start with, use the garden as a way to relax, not create another burden on your already busy life. This way you will continue to garden even if it later becomes a necessity.

When do you plant? I start when the ground is free of frost in the spring and quit before the first snow. In the spring, I plant lettuce in late February. My soil is sandy and drains well. I scratch up the surface and start with lettuce, spinach and snow peas. I continue with root crops, and by May Ist, I have most of my first plantings done. That may be too early for more northerly states and late for the southern states. I asked an old friend this question, and his advice was, "Son, if you don't lose some in the spring you aren't planting early enough. If you don't lose one in the fall, you quit too soon." The seed package tells you how long it will take for a crop to grow, let that guide be your guide.

At the time of a major disaster all available food sources will be depleted in a few days. People will start evacuating the big cities. You may choose to stay. If that is the case I hope you are prepared with a 60 to 90 day supply of food. Water and power will not last without someone to maintain it. You will need to rethink your location. For a garden to be useful, you still need soil, water and sunlight. You need tools to work the soil. The hardware store, garden center or shopping center is a good choice to go looking. You may find bags of potting soil or bags of dirt that can be moved to your location. Don't overlook fertilizer or plant food; they will help. This is when those stored garden seeds can make the difference. Potting soil is light and will not hold water. Soil is heavy and may hold too much water. If you can, mix them together. Soil has more plant food in it than potting soil. Plants need water, but they will drown if over watered. If you are using bags of soil split open at the top, be sure to punch holes in the bottom so excess water can drain out. A rooftop might be a good location. It has sunlight and rain and is out of sight of two-legged predators. Remember, you will need to get materials up to the roof and water from time to time. Fencing may be needed and netting used to keep the pigeons out, or in. Roast pigeons and fresh greens can make a good meal. If you have never prepared a meal from scratch or have no idea how to prepare a fish, bird or animals to cook, now is the time to learn. It's also important to know what parts are edible and what are not. I would try to have gardens in more than one location.

If one fails or is found, you have a back up. As in most things, you need to plan ahead. Start learning today about gardening. The whole family can learn together. Basic skills are needed to survive. Your likelihood of surviving will depend on what skills you already know. There are many gardening books out there. Some are very basic, a good place to start. Gardening shows on TV can inspire you. Go on the web and look for sites on gardening. Take a trip to the farmer's market, talk to the farmer. You might arrange a field trip to their farm. You don't have to be an expert, just knowledgeable enough to know where to start. You don't have to be a chef to cook an edible meal.

I am listing a couple of sites to get you started: www gardeners. com contains a great deal of information, a good source for raised-bed gardening. Try logging on to *"Kitchen Garden Planner"* to start or *"Emergency Essentials"* at *www.BePrepared*.com. There is information on lots of items including seeds packed for long-term storage. Look at www. MotherEarthNews.com. The April/May issue 2009 was a great issue on gardening. The magazine is always a good source of information. But, the most useful tool needed to survive is common sense.

Chapter Eleven

Raising Animals

This chapter and most of the ones to follow are to help you after the first thirty days of the disaster. The knowledge in the following chapters is of value to the people who will have had at least thirty days of food and water storage and have survived in their homes. At this point most of the other people who did not store food and water will be gone. The city is now yours to use.

Very few people in the city will have had the opportunity to raise animals before the city went into a state of emergency. People in the country raise animals all the time, because they have the room. In the city you are limited on space; how would you get rid of the waste? Most cities also have ordinances against raising animals within the city limits. You are, therefore, limited on your ability to raise your own animals in advance.

If you had at least a 30-day supply of food then you are probably still in your home, but most of the people in the city will have gone. They went somewhere that they had planned to go in the event of a disaster, or they just packed up and headed for the country hoping to find food. Or maybe they went to a shelter, if there are any. By this time FEMA, the Red Cross, the Government or the military should have set up shelters, and most of your neighbors will have had no choice but to have gone there because they either didn't have food storage, or they were killed in the riots, or are out there on their own trying to survive.

If you can raise animals, every pound of meat you eat will keep you from using your food storage so it will last longer. After everyone around you has left the city in search of food and assistance, you will have most of the city to yourselves. That means you can raise animals in other peoples' homes or apartments. There will be many abandoned buildings around as well. You will have the whole city as a resource, because you were able to stay in your home for the first thirty days.

Dogs:

I know, they are cute and lovable. They are also protein! Many people around the world eat dogs. Don't forget if you have a dog and you don't eat it for food, you will have to feed it. If you choose a dog breed and get one as a pet, you should get both a male and female so when a disaster comes you can breed more to eat.

Cats:

Cats take up less space but don't have as much meat on them as dogs. They are easy to breed and will breed with any other cat. Many people will not see cats as protein, and therefore there may be cats still running in the streets. One female cat can produce 1,000 times its weight in offspring each year.

Birds:

There is not much meat on a bird that you buy from a pet shop, maybe a parrot. But chickens are good to eat. They eat bugs and lay eggs. This should be you first choice. If you plan ahead you can order chicken online or go to a pet store. You can go to this web site: *http://www. pathtofreedom.com/pathproject/simpleliving/chickens.shtml.* It provides information for raising chickens in the city in small amounts of space.

You will not have running water by this time, so you can use the bathtub or shower as a place to raise the chickens. You can hatch some of the eggs for more chickens and eat the remainder of the eggs. As your flock grows you will have chicken to eat. Pigeons are a good source of protein. They are big enough to eat, and in the city there are many around. In a later chapter we will talk about trapping pigeons. You can eat the pigeon and then use the guts from the pigeon to trap rats.

Rats:

Everyone knows there are many rats in cities. They taste pretty good, but do not try to raise wild rats. They are full of diseases and often carry rabies. We will cover hunting and trapping rats in a later chapter, but you can find white rats at a pet store and raise them in your home.

Rabbits:

Yes it's true! They do multiply quickly. You can get them at a pet store, or you may be able to trap one. Raising rabbits are much cheaper, more efficient, and more productive than raising chickens. A doe can produce up to 1,000 times her body weight in food per year. Go to this web site for details: *http://www.i4at.org/lib2/rabbits.htm.*

Goats:

Goats are about the biggest animal you should try to raise in the city. But remember that by now the city is mostly empty, and you may be able to find an abandoned building. Or maybe the basement of the building you live in will work for raising goats. The best thing about goats is that they will eat almost anything, so you don't have to provide much food to raise them. Not only is goat meat good, but goats also give milk. The milk is good and high in fat. This could save your baby's life. Go to this web site for details: *http://goodbyecitylife.com/animals/goat.htm.*

Again planning is the most important part of all you do. You need to think about which of these animals you might want to raise and then read about how to raise them, find where you could get them and have the tools and equipment you may need. Look around and see where you might raise the animals, and buy in advance the fencing you may need or any other items you will need and don't currently have. It will be too late to get what is needed after the emergency begins.

Remember, though, if you have enough food storage you will not need to raise animals.

Chapter Twelve
Hunting – Trapping

The city has many more animals than most people realize. After the first 30 days and most of the population have gone, you have the city to yourself. Think of it as a big supply house. Most of the homes as well as businesses will be abandoned. Animals will quickly find their way into homes and buildings searching for food. With no one to keep the animals under control, they will multiply quickly. They will be inside buildings and easier to hunt and trap.

Here are some do's and don'ts and ideas on how to hunt and trap, but you need to go on the web or to a bookstore or library to get the details about what kind, and how to use, the different types of traps. The best thing you can do is to have some hands-on training. Look for local hunting clubs or NRA classes. Each state has a Department of Natural Resources with information about hunting and trapping.

At www.pipehitterstactical.com you can sign up for urban survival and many other classes that are intended for people in the city, and classes are held in big cities all over the U.S. Urban Survival also teaches a class on trapping and everything you will need to know with hands-on experience.

Cats – dogs – rats – squirrels – pigeons – raccoons – groundhogs/ woodchucks - Alligators – large snakes – large birds – fish – frogs – deer – coyote.

If you had sufficient food storage, you would not have to hunt or trap.

Humane Live Traps**:**
Some of you may think this is what you want because of your feelings about animals. Actually, you need to think again before you go out and buy humane live traps. The primary purpose of using humane live traps

is to trap animals for relocation. That is not what you are doing; you will be trapping the animals for food. I assure you that you will not like having to kill the cute little animal as he lies there helpless and trying to get away. If the temperature is above 32 degrees, then the animal will start to decay quickly and you will have to check your traps every few hours. The advantage of a live trap is that the animal will be alive and not start to decay until you kill it, and you don't have to check your traps as often as a quick kill trap. A disadvantage of the live trap, though, is that you could be bitten or clawed by the animal. You can get an infection from the bite, and there is no physician around to take care of it. More people in wars die from infections than from bullets. So if you use a live trap, you will need good gloves. The best way to kill the animal is with a gun. Having a gun in the city is not easy. A .22 handgun or pellet gun is the best thing to use for a quick kill. However, it makes a noise, and if you are on cement or a hard surface the bullet can go though the animal and bounce off the floor or wall and hit you or someone around you. A knife works well, but you have to hold the animal yourself to destroy it. You should not be dealing with large animals like cows and horses. I recommend a pellet gun. You can buy them at most Wal-marts, and they don't cost much. They don't make much noise and yet should be able to kill any of the animals on the above list except the alligator, or maybe large snakes like pythons, and deer.

We took a group of men on a survival-training mission. They had to live on the food that they could kill. I sent one to a pond to catch frogs, and when he came back I asked him where the frogs were. He said he had gotten 30 frogs but threw them back because he couldn't kill them. Two days later after not having food, the men went back to the pond and caught and killed the frogs and ate them.

We will go more into weapons in the chapter on weaponry.

<u>Quick kill traps</u>:
    Traps that kill the animals quickly will save you from having to handle live animals and getting bitten or clawed. However depending on the temperature, the animal will start to decay quickly so you will have to check your traps often. Any time the weather is above freezing you will have to check your traps within hours. But then you will not have a regular job, and it will be your job to provide food for yourself and others.

Homemade traps:

You are only limited by your imagination. For small birds like pigeons you can use a simple box trap. It can be wood or cardboard. Set it up with a stick about 10 inches long under one side with a string attached to the bottom of the stick and put some corn or anything birds eat under the box. Stand back at least 25 feet and wait until a pigeon is under the box, pull the string and the box falls over the pigeon. Now you still have to kill it, but you can eat the pigeon and use the pigeon guts to trap rats in the same manner.

You can use an old refrigerator. Have a string on the door and wait for an animal to go inside and then pull the door shut. You can lure an animal into a large room and trap it there, hang concrete blocks up and drop them on the animals.

Hunting:

If you have never hunted then you will not learn everything in detail here that you will need to know to go out and hunt. You need to learn hunting with hands-on experience. Take a course. The NRA gives great classes on hunting, and so do most state departments of natural resources. You can also sign up for training at *www.pipehitterstactical.com*.

NOTE: remember not to poison animals you are going to eat!

Weapons:

We will go into more detail on weaponry in a later chapter. We will cover weapons for hunting in this book, and we will cover weapons for personal protection in *Surviving a Hostile City II*.

Snakes:

Small snakes are no problem unless they are poisonous. But large snakes and poisonous snakes such as rattlesnakes are a different matter. Rattlesnakes and other poisonous snakes provide you with two problems: (1) how to kill them without getting bitten. Remember you can't call 911; no one will come and (2) when you prepare a poisonous snake, you must cut the head off back far enough so that you don't eat the poison gland.

Large but not poisonous snakes have their own special problem to deal with. They have a great deal more meat because they are so large. Make no mistake, the python has large teeth and is very fast. I was in Southeast Asia and came upon a 12-foot python stretched out on a tree limb about ten feet above the ground. I thought I could go up and grab his tail and throw him down to the others who were with me. I had no more then grabbed his tail when in an instant he had turned around and his face was in my face with his mouth wide open! I could feel the hot breath coming from his mouth. I fell out of the tree and shot the huge thing. Shooting them is best, but a 40-pound concrete block dropped on his head will do the job as well.

Cats, dogs and other small animals:
    Take a walk around the area where you live to watch and see what animals live nearby and where they run to hide. You need to watch at different times of the day. Some animals will only come out at dark and some only during the day. It is best to shoot those animals, however. You can trap them, but they make noise when they are in a trap unless it is a quick kill trap. A good pellet gun will work, not a BB gun. A .22 caliber gun is just about right for city hunting, but not much good for personal protection. A .22 with a suppressor is great for hunting. Later we will tell you how to buy a suppressor; yes, you can buy a suppressor.
    You will need a good light. The best is to have night vision. We will talk about where and how to buy night vision. Night vision is good for hunting, personal protection and scavenging.

Fish and Frogs:
    You will be surprised at how many places you can find fish and fogs. If you have a river or stream running though your city, there will most likely be fish and frogs there. Also think about some of the stores you have been in where fish were in some kind of glass display. Bright colored carp may live in some type of pond or display. You are right if you are thinking that carp don't taste good, but they are protein.
    If you search a pond or river you may have to go in after the fish or frogs, so you may want to have a skin diving mask and fins as well as a spear gun. You can use normal fishing tackle. You can use a net on a long pole; buy a net and duct tape it to a 10-foot piece of PVC plastic pipe.

    DUPONT WOBBLER! The best and quickest way to obtain fish in a pond or river is to use explosives. Yes, explosives. You can use fire works; some will go off under water, but some you will have to light in a bottle and throw into the water. In *Surviving A Hostile City II*, we will tell you how to make explosives, where to buy what you need and how to make them.

<u>Deer – coyote</u>**:**

Animals are good at adapting to their environment. When I go to a big city I usually spend time just looking around trying to see all the different animals there are in the city. When I was stationed in DC I was surprised how many deer I saw. Driving around the beltway it was not uncommon to see dead deer in the road. Out West I saw many coyotes and even big wild cats.

The good thing about all the animals that live in the city is that they hide from all the people. Yes, that is good, because after 30 days and most of the people are gone the animals will be free to come out and feed. Also, cats and dogs left behind will multiply quickly. Cats will basically be wild animals and will be finding food on their own so you will not have to provide food for them.

However it is hard to trap deer and large game. We have tried it; if you trap a deer and it is still alive, you are going to have to shoot it. Their hooves can cut you and break bones, and a blow to your head could kill you. If you are going after deer and large game then you need a large caliber weapon.

At *www.pipehitterstactical.com* you can see a video of someone fighting and killing a deer with only a knife.

Chapter Thirteen

Preparing Animals for Cooking

There are many do's and don'ts when preparing animals for cooking. It would take a thousand pages to cover them all. This is not a detailed "how to" book. We will cover basics. However, if you have never killed, field dressed an animal (removing the guts and lungs and heart), then you will need more than this book or any book. You can go to the web site *http://www.gunnersden.com/index.htm.hunting-game-processing. html.* for the information you need to learn. You can buy books with detail on how to prepare animals for cooking. The best thing to do is obtain hands-on training. Most states' departments of natural resources have training on trapping and skinning. Look around and you may find a conservation club. You may have a chicken that has already been cleaned, but you need to learn how to cut it up into smaller parts. You can try to contact a local grocery store or butcher shop to see if they may be willing to show you how to cut meat.

Basics:
Remember that high temperatures are the enemy. The moment the animal dies, the meat starts to decay. The higher the temperature, the faster it decays. Here is the basic concept for preparing an animal: first, remove all the internal parts and drain the blood.

You will then need to remove the hair or feathers or scales.

We have been overseas a great deal, and in most third world countries you can see dead animals hanging in open-air markets with flies and bugs crawling all over them. Some of this meat hangs there for hours. That is why most of those countries have a high mortality rate. It is important to cook the animal as quickly as possible. Make sure you cook it all the way through so there is no blood in the meat.

This is a topic that could be discussed at great length, but if you are going to be involved in hunting and trapping and skinning of animals, then you need hands-on training. The information given here is not enough for you to know how to go out and skin an animal and cook it.

Meat is hard to store. If you live in a cold climate, and it is the cold season of the year, that will help. Otherwise, you will have to dry the meat or cook and eat it right away.

Remember, if preparing animals to eat is not what you want to do to survive, start storing your food.

Chapter Fourteen

Weaponry

There are two basic needs for weapons. One is to provide you with food, and the second is to protect yourself. In this book we are only going to talk about using firearms to provide you with food. In **Surviving A Hostile City II** we will cover in detail what you need to know for self-defense. Be sure to check the laws in your area pertaining to guns and knives.

This book is meant for people who live in cities, and because of the laws in cities, we will try to guide you on how to be prepared and stay within the laws of most large cities.

Chemical:

There is not much need for chemical weapons when it come to hunting animals, but chemicals will be covered in detail in the book on self-defense, **Surviving A Hostile City II**. However, even with animals, you can use mace, pepper spray and other chemicals on cats, dogs and other animals to keep them at bay, or disorientate them in order to kill them for food. One of the best chemical sprays is wasp spray. This will do a better job on animals and humans than pepper spray, and it sprays up to 20 feet away. With this spray, you can hit an animal or a person in the eyes. You should have wasp spray in your home and in your 72-hour kit at all times. You should buy some and try it so you can see how far it can spray.

Knives:

Most cities and states have laws pertaining to knives and how long the blades can be, however, I cannot remember a time when I heard of anyone being arrested just for carrying a knife. You might be arrested if you have a large knife and are walking down the street of a large city, but for the most part, the laws regarding knives are not enforced. Most of the knives in your kitchen are too long according to the law. Most twelve year-old Boy Scouts have and carry knives.

You can go to almost any sporting goods store or a Wal-mart and buy large knives.

There is not an all in one knife that will suit your needs. A knife good for skinning is not going to be good for many of the other things you will to do with a knife. A box cutter is a good knife to have around. You can cut string, or plastic and open boxes, but it will not do a good job for skinning. We think you should have at least four types of knives: a box cutter, a good jackknife to have with you at all times, a knife with at least a six-inch blade that is strong enough to skin animals and clean fish, and a knife with at least a 12-inch blade to cut brush. You should also have an ax for cutting wood or 2 X 4's. You should have more than one set of your knives. This will allow you to keep one set in your 72- hour emergency kit and one set in your house. You should not use those knives until you need them. Keep them sharp and in good shape for when you do need them. And, don't forget to store something to sharpen them. Again, sit and talk to each other and think about what all you will need a knife for and then buy what you think you need. **Surviving A Hostile City II** will go into using knives for self-defense and as weapons.

Blowguns**:**

Like knives there are little or no laws pertaining to blowguns. They are cheap to buy, and you can practice with them in your home using a target made of cardboard. Blowguns can be used for killing rats, pigeons, cats, and small dogs for food. I have killed rabbits and squirrels with a blowgun. Becoming good with a blowgun will require a great deal of practice, but you can sit round your living room and watch TV while you practice.

Air Rifles**:**

Again, there are little or no laws regarding air rifles even in most cities. There may be laws about where you can shoot them, but not pertaining to the right to own them and keep them in your house or place of business. A good air rifle will cost from $59 to $159. The ammo is cheap, and you don't have to sign for it to buy it. Like the blowgun, you can practice with an air rifle in your home. It is much more powerful than a blowgun, and you will need a much sturdier target. You will have to be very careful when practicing with one. You can find targets at the stores where air rifles are sold, or you can use a homemade target. Stores sell air rifles that are .17 caliber and .22 caliber. This is the same size bullet that a regular .22 rifle shoots. The only difference is the speed of the bullet. A regular .22 is much faster than the air rifle, but the air rifle can travel at up to 1,100 feet a second. This gives the air rifle the power to kill larger animals at a longer range than a blowgun. The extra range is important. Also, air rifles make very little noise compared to a regular gun. There is no explosive charge in the air rifle, and the bullet doesn't travel faster than the speed of sound so there is little noise. I have killed small game with an air rifle. You could kill raccoons and other animals of that size. Remember to be careful, you could kill a human if you hit them in the right spot. You can go to a big box store like Wal-mart and buy an air rifle, take it home and learn to shoot it on your own, but you may buy the wrong one. We recommend you go to a store that primarily carries air rifles and paint ball guns. The dealer will show you the difference in the rifles, and most have indoor ranges to try them out before you buy. ***Surviving A Hostile City II*** will cover using an air rifle for self-defense.

<u>Bows and Cross-bows</u>**:**

These are good for city use, because there are little or no laws when it comes to bows. Bows are more powerful and have a longer range than air rifles. They can bring down larger game as well as humans. Bows cost more and take much more practice, however, and your home may not be large enough for you to practice with a bow. You may have to find a place to practice. Arrows can cost from $5 to $20 each, so if you miss and hit something hard and break the arrow, it can be costly. This is true not only for practice, but when you are in the city hunting in a building, and you miss and hit a wall, you may break your arrow and run out of arrows.

There are long bows, recurve bows, compound bows and crossbows. As you go up the list of bows, you move up in power, accuracy and cost. A long bow will not have as much power or range. A recurve bow has more power and range but costs more. It is also the hardest to pull and hold back when shooting. A good compound bow will cost in the hundreds of dollars. However, it has a great deal of power and is not as hard to pull back and hold. It is easier to learn to shoot and is more accurate. The crossbow is nice in that it is short, making it easier to store and carry. There are crossbows with scopes on them. In some states older hunters and disabled people are allowed to hunt with crossbows, because one doesn't have to be strong to pull it back. It is fast and will kill at a good range but costs a great deal of money compared to other bows. The arrows are also costly. Crossbows can cost up to $1,000.

If you are thinking about buying a bow, you should not go to a big box store; you should go to a sporting goods store or a gun and bow shop. Most good bow shops will be glad to talk to you and show you the difference between the bows, and they will have an indoor range for you to try out bows to see the difference and find out what you like and don't like. These are unlike the air rifle. You can go to a box store and buy an air rifle, take it home and learn how to use it. But, with a bow, you should try it out to be sure you buy the right one and take lessons, if possible.

Firearms:

A firearm is a weapon that uses some type of explosion to propel a bullet. Because the firearm uses explosives, it moves the bullet fast. It is the speed of a bullet that makes it deadly. If I took a bullet out of a round of ammo and threw it at you, it would not do much to you. But if I take that same bullet and shoot it at you at 3,000 feet per second, it will do lots of damage. So, it is the speed, not the weight of the bullet that kills. It is weight times speed that equals energy, and it is energy that does the damage.

Safety – Safety – Safety!

Before you buy or use any firearm, you need to take a safety and instruction course for firearms. You may need to take a course before you can buy a firearm in your area. But for your safety and the safety of your family and friends, you need to know how to use a firearm before you buy or use one.

Black Powder:

In most cities and states there are very few laws when it comes to black powder firearms. Even the ATF has very few laws when it comes to someone owning one. Even people, who are convicted criminals and can't own a regular firearm, can own and hunt with a black powder firearm. In most states, you don't need a license to own or carry a black powder firearm. Over the road truckers carry black powder firearms because there are few laws covering carrying them from state to state like there are with non-black powder firearms. **Be sure to check in your town, city and state to make sure about the laws on black powder firearms where you live before purchasing them.**

Because black powder doesn't burn as fast as non-black powder explosives, the bullet does not travel as fast so it doesn't have as much energy. Also, you have to load black powder firearms in a different way than non-black powder firearms. With a black powder firearm you load the powder and the bullet separately, so it will be slower to load and reload. You have to measure the powder and then use a rod or some type of device to push the bullet into the barrel. Black powder guns also cost much less to buy than a regular firearm.

Make no mistake! A black powder firearm will kill a human and big game. People hunt elk, bear and big game in Africa with black powder firearms. Many a person has been killed with a black powder firearm. All the soldiers had in the Revolutionary War and the Civil War was black powder. Black-powder firearms killed tens of thousands of people. So, it will kill anything you will be coming across. Then why is it not as good as a regular firearm? It is slow to load and reload. You also have to keep the black powder in a dry and cool place, and it is hard to load in snow and rain. It doesn't move the bullet as fast or as far. If you are using a 150-grain bullet, and you move it at 1,500 feet per second in a black powder firearm compared to 150-grain bullet moving at 3,000 feet per second out of a regular firearm, you can see that the energy and range would greatly increase. However, because the laws in big cities, and the cost of using regular firearms may restrict you, you may want to buy the black powder firearm.

Black Powder Handgun versus Black Powder Rifle and Shotgun:
Handguns may be single shot or they may hold up to six shots in a cylinder. You can shoot six times without reloading compared to a rifle. You have to load a rifle from the barrel, and it will only hold one shot at a time. Then you have to reload. The handgun has a short barrel, so you can carry it and hide it easily, but the shorter the barrel the shorter the range and speed of the bullet. So, the rifle will shoot farther and be more accurate.

There are also shotguns that use black powder. This firearm shoots a group of BB's rather than one bullet, so it is good for hunting small game. You don't have to be as accurate to hit your target. All black powder weapons make a great deal of noise and smoke and have a good kick to them. They come in many calibers, from small to large enough to take down an elephant. Again think about where you are going to be, the area around you and what size of game you will be hunting. Now go to a black powder gun store and talk to them about what you need. Get some training and practice before you buy the firearm you want.

Regular Firearms:
I want to remind you again how important it is to have training before you start to use a firearm. There are many types and calibers of firearms. There is not one firearm that will fit all your needs. Because of the cost, you may only want one, so we will try to help you pick the one that is best for you.

58

There are handguns, rifles and shotguns. Non-black powder firearms use self-contained rounds. That means that the bullet and powder are all in the same round, and all you need to do is load the cartridge into the firearm to be ready to shoot.

Handguns:

A handgun has a short barrel and is easy to carry and conceal. It doesn't have a long range, however, and the shorter the barrel the slower the bullet and the less energy the bullet will have. It will be harder to aim and hit the target. A normal handgun can hold from one round to 30 rounds and even more with some special magazines.

Handguns can be single action or double action revolvers where you load rounds into a cylinder that rotates as you fire. Some are single action; you have to cock the hammer each time to fire. Double action means all you have to do is pull the trigger to fire. Some are semi-auto. This means the firearm will fire each time you pull the trigger, and the rounds are fed by placing a magazine in the pistol.

Rifles:

Rifles have longer barrels and therefore a longer range with more energy. They are easier to aim but are larger and heavier to carry and hard to conceal. Rifles can hold from one to 100 rounds and even more with special magazines. There are all kinds of rifles: break open, lever action, pump action, bolt action. Those are the ways that you can insert the round into the chamber. You can buy a .22 for under $100 or pay up to thousands for a rifle. The price may be for better quality, or it may be for gold inlay that will have no affect on the performance of the rifle. In most states a rifle has to have a 16-inch barrel to be legal.

Shotguns:

Shotguns are larger firearms. Most are good for hunting because they shoot many BB's in one shot that spreads out and covers a wide area. It is easier to hit a target with a shotgun, but it is a short-range firearm compared to a rifle. These come in break open, lever action, bolt action, pump-action, single shot or semi auto with up to a 20-round magazine, long barrel or short barrel. A shotgun needs to have an 18-inch barrel to be legal.

Ammos:

For handguns and rifles there are many calibers and kinds of ammo from a .22 that is .22 of an inch in diameter and a 30 grain bullet used to kill small game at short range, to a 50 caliber BMG that is .50 of an inch in diameter and the bullet weighs 800 grains and will go though a car engine at a mile.

There are many bullets and case sizes, and all have advantages and disadvantages.

Bullets can be full metal jacket; they will travel fast and accurately for long distances. They will stay in tact and go though most targets. There are hollow point bullets that have a hole in the tip. When they hit the target they will spread and cause a large hole and do a lot of damage, but do not travel as far or as accurately. There are many types of bullets and powder charges. Different bullets and powder charges can be used for hunting in different areas and to hunt different game.

ATF or BATF (Alcohol – Tobacco - Firearms or Bureau of Alcohol – Tobacco – Firearms):

This is the U.S. Government's law enforcement agency for firearms and explosives.

You can buy and own Class 3 and Class 2 weapons. There are full auto machine guns, rifles and shotguns that are too short to buy and suppressors that will require you to go through the ATF in order to have the right to purchase. This takes time and money, but you can buy those firearms.

General Overview:

We have covered the very basics on firearms. If you are thinking about buying and using firearms, you need to read about them and take a training course. Again, don't go to a Wal-mart to buy firearms, go to a gun store. Tell the dealer you don't know what to buy and explain what you want to use it for. Most dealers will be glad to help. Where we live, when a person comes into a local gun store and has never owned a firearm, most of the time the dealers send them to us first for training. Buyers often find out that they would have purchased the wrong firearm. They would have bought what they saw on TV or what a friend told them to buy. I have friends who have been hunting and shooting all their lives, and they are still doing it wrong and are not safe because they started out wrong. I don't hunt or shoot with them, because I know they are unsafe. I have been in five wars and have never shot anything or anyone that I didn't want to. I have never had an accident with a firearm, nor has my son who has been all over the world carrying firearms. Lorna is also an accomplished hunter and security officer, competent with all types of firearms. She also has never lost control of a round. She learned, trained, and we all keep up on our training to be proficient and safe with our firearms. Firearms and ammo cost a great deal of money, and you need to have the one that is best for you and best for what you are going to do.

This book is written for people who live in cities and who are going to use firearms to hunt. I think you should consider owning a good .22 rifle. It doesn't cost much, and the ammo is cheap. We use .22 conversion in some of our firearms to practice, because it costs less for the ammo. The .22 will take most of the small game you will be encountering in a city. It will take everything up to a deer. Or, you may also want to consider a 410 shotgun. You will not have to be as good of a shot with a 410 to take game, and it will fire both shot and single bullet slugs to take animals like deer.

If you are in an area where there is larger game such as deer, elk or bear, then you will need a much larger firearm. A 308 or 30-06 would be a good firearm for larger game. The .22, 410, 308 and 30-06 use commonly found ammo.

It is a whole different matter when we talk about using guns for self-defense. That is why we will publish **Surviving A Hostile City II**, which is dedicated to self-defense.

Read magazines like **"Guns and Ammo"** and **"American Rifleman,"** and watch the outdoor channels on cable. But most importantly, get some training. You can log on to the web to locate these classes. We also provide training around the country about everything discussed in this book. Contact us for hands-on training. Email *lornadare@live.com* or *Kaalwood@hotmail.com*. Or you can go online at *www.pipehitterstactical. com* to find class information.

Chapter Fifteen

Fuel & Fuel Storage

There are four main reasons for fuel:
- Heat
- Cooking
- Light
- Transportation

Some of the fuels will fulfill more than one of your needs.

Fuels and energy will be the items that you will have the most trouble with storing in quantities you will need. In normal times some people don't have enough money to have all the fuels and energy they need even when there is enough out there. Liquid fuel is hard to store, it is dangerous, most of it smells, it doesn't store well and needs to be rotated every few months. It takes up a great deal of room. As we have seen all over the world in wars and natural disasters, there is never enough fuel to be found. The Government will come in and take control of what fuel there is. Even Para-military forces or rebels in a war zone never have enough fuel and have to fight for it. Trucking companies and farmers don't store a year's supply of fuel, even though they have the money and facilities to do so.

You are going to be lucky to be able to store 10% of the fuels that you need.

Surviving a Hostile City II will teach you how to use force to both defend and acquire fuels, but here we will go over some of the fuels and talk about the advantages and disadvantages. It would be wise to store your fuels in containers marked "poison" or hazardous material" to keep people away from your fuel sources.

Gasoline:
In an emergency it will be hard to obtain gasoline, so it would be wise to store some. However, if you have your food storage and are staying

in place, or you don't have a vehicle, then you may not want or need to store gasoline. But, even if you don't need it for your own use, it will be a valuable item for trading.

Gasoline is one of the more flammable liquids, and you must be careful where and how you store it. For safety, don't store it in or near where you are living. However, you will have to think of security wherever you store it, as it will be valuable. If you intend to store it and use it in a motor then you will need chemicals that will extend its life. Most gasolines will lose octaine over a year, so it may not run an engine after a year's time. Gasoline smells, and people will be able to smell it and locate it. if you have a vehicle, don't keep much in the tank because people will steal it from your vehicle. You can use it to produce heat, light or run engines, but it needs to be rotated every few months or you will need to add an additive to keep the octain high enough to run engines.

Kerosene:

This is also going to be hard to find. Most kerosene, like gasoline, is stored in underground tanks. Without power it is going to be hard to get to. Because it has so many uses, many people will be after it. Kerosene will be one of the substances people will fight to get and to keep.

Both gasoline and kerosene can also be used for weapons. In *Surviving a Hostile City II* we will explain how to use fuels for weapons.

Kerosene is safer than gas to store and use. Kerosene is also the same as diesel fuel, and it is what is used in jet planes. J4 and jet fuel are grades of kerosene. Many camping stoves run on kerosene. It will last longer in storage for use in heating and cooking, but like gas, it also doesn't store well as a fuel for vehicles. When it turns cold outside, it will get thick and does not burn well. That is why you see many big trucks left running at a truck stop in the winter to keep the temperature up, and most of them have fuel heaters. Kerosene doesn't explode as easily as gas, however, and is safer to store. A kerosene heater for your home will use about one gallon of fuel every five hours. You will need a great deal fuel for heating and cooking.

Lamp Oil:

Today, just as in Pioneer days, the use of wick lamps for lighting will be an important asset during times when there is no electricity. Lamp oil is plentiful, cost-effective and easy to store.

LP Gas (LP = liquefied petroleum gas):
This is both butane and propane. It is stored in metal containers under pressure. You have to store it in the pressurized containers. It burns clean but can explode if near heat or is hit with a bullet. You must have the right equipment to refill your tanks, and the tanks are heavy. It comes in all sizes of containers from 12 oz. to 1,000 gallons and larger. It can be used for cooking, heating or to run lights or generators. It can be used to repair pipes and as a torch to solder and make repairs. LP gas has many uses, but it takes up a great deal of room and is heavy to move.

Wood:
Wood requires tools to be cut and split. It takes up a great amount of space and can be a hiding and breeding place for insects. You need a stove or fireplace in which to burn the wood; you can't just burn wood in the living room. Wood is costly to buy and has to be hauled into your location. You need something with a good chimney to burn the wood. This is harder to cook on, because it is hard to control the temperature of the burning wood.

Charcoal:
You can buy and store charcoal, but you need to keep it dry or it will be hard to get started. You have to be careful, because charcoal will kill you if you burn it in a confined area. You must burn it outside, on a porch or in a garage with the overhead door open. You can cook with charcoal, but it is hard to heat an area because it has to be used in an open area to be safe. Charcoal doesn't give off any light, so its only real purpose is for cooking.

Candles – Matches:
Both candles and matches are easy to get and don't cost much. You should buy as many of those products as you can. Remember to store the matches in some kind of waterproof container or in a cool dry place.

Batteries:
Batteries are not cheap. There are many kinds of batteries. You need to read the labels and see how long their storage life is and if they are rechargeable, but it takes some type of other power to recharge them. There will most likely not be any electricity.

Generators – Fuel-Run and Manual:

Generators come in all sizes; the larger the unit and the more power it generates, the more fuel it uses. So, bigger may not be better. You may want to have two generators. A larger one can be used to run more things in your home such as your heat and refrigerator. A generator is good for saving your food, but it will use up much of your fuel. You might want a small generator that can charge your batteries or run one thing at a time, but will use less fuel.

You can obtain generators that run on gas, diesel, and natural gas. If you are going to stay where you are, you may want to set up a generator and hook it to whatever fuel your home is on, LP or natural gas. Then you won't have to store and carry large amounts of gas. If you have LP gas at your house, then you may have, or can set up, a larger tank, so you don't have to worry about getting so much LP gas at a later date.

You should look into purchasing a manual generator. There are small ones that you can crank in order to run or charge your cell phone, and there are larger ones that you can operate with your hands or feet to provide power like your fuel-powered generator.

Solar:

You can buy small solar panels to charge batteries and larger ones to power larger equipment. These cost a great deal, and they take up a great deal of space. You can buy or make solar ovens for baking.

Overview:

We want to state again that you will need and use more energy than you can and will store. It takes a great deal of fuel to produce heat, and that alone will eat up most of your fuel and energy. This is going to be the biggest challenge in your storage program. As we have gone around the world in war zones, fuel is always a problem. The best way to deal with your fuel needs is to do what we teach and do in a war zone –

You re-supply off your enemy, or whoever is out there! Again, in *Surviving a Hostile City II*, we will teach you how to re-supply off others.

Chapter Sixteen

Currency

What is currency? It is anything you have that is worth something to someone else.

When hard times come and the system breaks down, history has shown that paper money and coins (coins with value that are dependent on the Government's backing but have no value because of what they are made of, such as gold or silver) that are used day to day to do business are one of the first things to lose their value.

In 1849, many people moved West to get rich in the gold rush, but very few got rich from gold. There were many who became rich or made money off the gold miners by selling them food, horses, and tools. Remember, in chaos there is profit.

When you are out scavenging, keep your eyes open for all kinds of things. You may find items you already have or don't need because you were prepared, but most people will not be prepared or have what they need such as a chain, a piece of rope, a hammer. You could use all of this as currency.

Gold:

Gold has always kept its value in the past, and it looks like it will still be of value in hard times because most governments will accept it as payment. Gold in coins or bars is good because people know the purity of it. Most coins are from 98 to 99% pure, and this is the same with bars. You will have to be careful about gold jewelry, however. You will not be able to tell by looking how pure the gold is; it can be gold-plated or as much as 24 carat, which is pure gold. Nevertheless, gold should be a good currency in hard times. The only thing that will be difficult, however, is that a one-ounce coin is worth about $1,200 right now in 2010, and you may have to cut it up into smaller pieces. You may only want to trade for a gallon of fuel and won't want to spend $1,200 for it, but you may have to. However, you can't count on how much gold would be worth at that time; it may be worth much more if paper money becomes worthless, or it may be that you need food and without much food around you may have to give an ounce of gold for a loaf of bread. Think about that. If you have nothing to eat how much would you want for the bread that you have? It will not have a set value; it will be worth what people want for what they have just as you will set the price for the things you have that other people will want. You might want to think about buying gold now. It is high in cost, but ask yourself do you think the price of gold will be higher or lower in a year? We think it will be higher. Secondly, even if gold doesn't increase in cost, will you be better off when the system falls apart to have gold to trade or the paper money you have now? Again, we believe you will be better off with gold. Don't think of it just as an investment to make money, but as an investment to save what you have. Remember, you may be able to trade for a weapon with an ounce of gold that doesn't take up much weight or space.

Silver:

Silver is going to be similar in worth to gold, except we believe it is going to be better for trading. This is because an ounce of silver is worth about $18 an ounce right now in 2010. So, it is going to be easier to trade for small things or things in small quantities. You may be able to trade for a loaf of bread or a gallon of gas easier with an ounce of silver than an ounce of gold. I think silver is going to be good for trading, but you will need a great deal of it, which will weigh a lot. Right now it will take 60 ounces of silver to be worth one ounce of gold. That is 3.75 pounds of silver to carry around or hide for the same value as one ounce of gold. A good thing about silver over gold, however, is that you can afford to buy silver with less money. You may be able to save and buy one ounce of silver a month at $20.00, but it would take sixty months to save enough money to buy one ounce of gold. It is better to get it as soon as you can and **keep it a secret.**

Other Precious Metals, Diamonds and Gems:

There are many other metals, diamonds and gems out there to buy, and they may be a good investment. We are not financial advisors in anyway. We don't advise you to buy or keep any of these for your survival storage. It is hard enough to tell if gold and silver is real or not, and very few people will know how to tell if platinum is real or how pure it is. This is the same with diamonds; you will have to ask a jeweler to know if diamonds are real, and then you would have to know how to grade them. Because of this, most people will not want to trade in anything exotic like platinum or diamonds.

Remember that when the system falls apart, people such as bankers, stockbrokers and jewelers will be in bad shape because they will not be prepared. They will most likely be depending on their money and credit cards to survive, and they will be trying to trade their money and valuables for food and water. If you have food and water storage, you may wind up with their gold, silver and valuables.

Food-Water:

If you have food storage, not only will you survive, but if you store it correctly you can be in command of everything. All around the world the people who control the food and water control the people.

In WW II, people had ration books in the United States. Things have not changed much as far as what will be in demand during a disaster. As you buy your food storage you should keep in mind that others will need the same things. When you have extra money, or items are on sale, you should buy more than you need to save for trading. When people are hungry they will buy or trade anything for food of any kind. Coffee, beans or anything you can afford, will be worth more than money when there is no food.

We will talk more about security of your food in **Surviving A Hostile City II**, but extra food may save your life in more ways than just to have it to eat.

The bottom line is that food will be the best currency you can have during a disaster. Whatever you pay for food now, it will be worth many times more than what you paid for it. Don't forget that you will never lose any money buying food; the worst thing that can happen is you can eat it and not replace it in your storage. If chaos doesn't come, you may need your food storage if you lose your job. I have known people who have lost their jobs and lived off their food storage until they found another job.

Don't forget to buy and store seeds to grow food. Seeds don't take up much space and are not costly. Place the seeds in plastic bags you can seal, and store them in a cool dry place. The best types of seeds are non-hybrid seeds, but any type is better than none. The best types are corn, tomatoes, potatoes, all kinds of beans, mostly items that have a short growing time. These are good for trading, too, so buy more than you think you will need.

Tobacco – Coffee - Sugar – Chocolate:

These items need to be in their own group because each has a special place in an emergency as trading items.

Tobacco. Everyone knows the health risks of using tobacco. However, because it is so addictive and does seem to have a medical value when it comes to helping some people release stress, it is important. In an emergency there is even more stress than a person will normally experience. In POW camps, cigarettes are one of the major items of value to trade. In Vietnam we had three cigarettes in each C-ration, and as a non-smoker I was able to trade them for food to both soldiers and the locals. We are non-smokers, but we store tobacco products to trade.

Coffee. Think of how many cups of coffee you drink a day or how many people around you start their day with a cup of coffee. I have heard people say when they are down emotionally or tired or have had a bad day, that they need a cup of coffee. Coffee is a stimulant and it really does help people stay awake and be more alert. People believe it helps, also, and because of that it does. Again there will be a great deal of stress in an emergency, and the need for stimulants such as coffee will be in great demand. It is best to store strong, non-decaffeinated coffee. In a time of stress and emergency, the stimulant part of coffee will be what makes it so valuable.

Sugar. During World War II ration stamps were used, and sugar was on the list. I remember my mother saying she never had enough sugar. It gives quick energy and can make some foods taste better. It may help young people to eat some of the foods in your storage that may not taste good. It is easy to store and doesn't cost much. I just paid $2.50 for a 5 lb. bag to put in our storage. You can just put it in a zip lock bag, or anything to keep it dry and keep the insects out. If the sugar turns hard, that's not a problem. You can just chip some off and dissolve it in water or in your cup of coffee. If the sugar becomes infested with insects you can run it though a filter. We take the 5 lb. bag and put it in a zip lock bag. Then we put the zip lock bag in a one-gallon paint can that you can buy anywhere and put the lid on it. It will store well for years.

Chocolate. This is a form of sugar, energy and a stimulant. It also has attributes that sugar doesn't have that are of value. Cocoa solids contain alkaloids such as theobromine and phenethylamine, which have physiological effects on the body. It has been linked to serotonin levels in the brain. Some researchers found that chocolate, eaten in moderation, can lower blood pressure and produces pleasant emotions. You can melt it and use it as a topping to make food taste better. Lorna believes chocolate should be its own food group. It makes her happy in a way that sugar doesn't. During a time of emergency, it would be better to hand out a piece of chocolate than to hand out sugar. Chocolate is also easy to store. We store it just like we do sugar, in zip lock bags inside a paint can. If it gets cold that is all right, and if it gets hot and melts, that will not damage it. Just break off a piece and eat it. However, it does cost more per pound than sugar.

We recommend you store a great deal of these items like tobacco, coffee and chocolate. Store more than you will need. Overseas or at hurricane sites, those items were the most valuable for trade. Also, you can't have too much; you can always eat it. It will not go to waste.

Weapons and Improvised Weapons:

Weapons become the second most valuable items when there is a problem. We have been all over the world in times of war and natural disasters. Every time food was the number one most valuable item and weapons were second. With weapons you can defend your food or fight to get more food. Again, in *Surviving A Hostile City II*, we will discuss in detail how to both defend and fight for food.

Most of the time when we are talking about weapons, we are referring to firearms or bows and arrows. Para-weapons are items that you don't normally use for weapons but could. These may be what you use to hunt animals, such as knives and air rifles. There are many things in and around your home that can be used for weapons from the chemicals under you sink to the tools you use to make repairs. A rock in a sock will kill quickly. In *Surviving A Hostile City II*, we will teach you how to make and use the items in and around your house to protect yourself.

Just remember that anything you can use as a weapon, others can, also, and if they don't have them and you do, you have the upper hand. This becomes currency to you.

Medical Supplies:

Medical supplies fall some where between second and third on the list of valuable items. If you and your group are in good health, and no one is injured, then it will not be as valuable to you as to a group who has sick or injured people. Medical supplies may move to the number one position for them. Think about what you would do right now if ten people came to your house and all needed medical attention. Maybe they all just fell down, and you had to deal with nothing more than small cuts or minor injuries. How much tape, alcohol or gauze do you have? Remember that there is not going to be an EMT coming to help you or a hospital to travel to for care. Add to this the fact that in a disaster, everyone will be doing many more physical things that can lead to accidents. People will be doing more things they will not be adept at doing. You can't do much about storing prescription drugs (refer to the chapter on medical), but you should buy large quantities of items such band-aids, ace bandages, alcohol, aspirins, tape (duct tape as well as medical tape), gauze, sterile water, anti-diarrhea medications, sun block and anti-bacterial cream. A non-electronic thermometer and a manual blood pressure kit are necessities. If you only have one of those items, or just enough for your own use, then these cannot be used as currency; they are only a part of your storage. Only if you have two or more of the items, or more than what you need, do they become currency. Most people rely on the local medical unit to take care of them, or they run down to the local store to get what they need when they need it. In a disaster, you will be the local store with high prices. Most of those items take up a small amount of space and don't cost much, but they will save many lives and will be worth a great deal.

Infections will kill or disable more of you than anything else. You can buy most of these items for very little money at Wal-mart. A good place to purchase items such as alcohol and tape is a dollar store of some kind. Generic aspirins are just fine to use; you can never have enough aspirin on hand.

You will be able to set your price or trade for what you need; someone will need medical supplies.

Tools and Supplies:

Following a catastrophic event, there will not be repairmen for you to call to repair things, so you will need tools to repair items yourself. You may have to repair many items from your vehicle to the windows or the hinges on the door. In cities, many people live in apartments or rented homes of some type, and they don't do much of their own maintenance or repairs. Older people also don't make many repairs. Many people will have a hard time finding a hammer or screwdriver to make repairs with, and since most people don't work on their own vehicles, they don't have the tools needed for that. You may not have the skills to work on your own vehicle, but you may be able to trade something you have to someone else to repair your vehicle. If you have the tools, you will be ahead of everyone else. So, you should have tools needed to repair as many kinds of things as you can. You may be able to trade the use of your tools for something you need or need done. You don't need to spend a great deal of money on tools, and I would not recommend that you buy new tools. However stores like Harbor Freight have new tools at a good price. The best place to purchase tools is at a pawnshop. You can buy good tools at a hundredth of their value. A good time to buy tools is when the building trade is down or in the northern United States when it is cold. Much of the construction slows down in the winter, and laborers pawn their tools because they are out of work.

You may or may not have power during a disaster, so invest most of your money in hand tools. A hand drill has come in very handy when we were in a part of the world during a time of war and there was no power. This is the same for air tools. It takes some form of power to run most air tools. Some run off compressed air tanks, and others need powered compressors. It is good if you buy extra compressed air tanks.

You may be able to get a good buy on a generator or batteries for tools at a pawnshop.

Don't forget to stock nails, screws and repair parts. You can't repair or replace something even if you have tools if you don't have the parts. Think about the items that have broken down in your life, and try to have as many of those kinds of parts on hand as you can. If you have parts and tools, then you again will have a form of currency!

<u>Knowledge</u>:

Your medical supplies will be worth a great deal, but think about how much more they will be worth if you have some knowledge of how to use your medical supplies.

Tools to repair a car are good, but again, how much more will they be worth if you also know how to repair the car?

Manuals and "how to" books will be of great value. Books on how to store food or cans will also be of value. You cannot count on having power, so books on tape, CD's or DVD's may not be as valuable as hard copies of the material. You can go to used bookstores and find "how to" books for as little as 50 cents or a dollar. Think of their value when someone needs them. Books about first aid and herbal medicine will be of great value to both you and others. You can also find a great deal of information on the web to print off and make a file. Make extra copies to use to trade or sell. Again, books turn into currency.

Your personal knowledge will be as good as gold. Learn as much as you can about everything you can that may be of value to yourself or others in a crisis. Take a Red Cross CPR class. Many cities hold these classes, and so does Home Land Security. They give classes in every state, and most of these classes are free. These classes are about many subjects you need to know. This will also give you knowledge on how the Government works and is going to be of help to you in an emergency. All this knowledge will be something you may be able to trade or sell during a time of chaos.

Fuels:

I don't consider fuels as currency. I know what you are thinking – everyone will need fuel. There will not be enough, so it will be worth a great deal. Therefore, it is a currency. While it is true that there will not be enough fuel around, and everyone will need and want it, there will not be enough of it to sell. What there is will be hard to get to and hard to store. Fuel is dangerous, most of it smells, it doesn't store well and needs to be rotated every few months. It also takes up a great deal of space. As we have seen all over the world in wars and natural disasters, there is never enough fuel around. The Government will come in and take control of what fuel there is. In WW II, our military had to stop at times because it ran out of fuel. The Germans ran out of fuel for their planes. Even Para military forces, or rebels in a war zone, never have enough fuel and have to fight for it. You are going to be lucky to be able to store 10% of the fuel you need.

An item is only currency when you have more than you need and can afford to trade or sell it to others. It is very unlikely you will have enough fuel for yourself, let alone extra to sell or trade. If you only have enough for yourself, then it is not currency. It is a part of your storage.

You may be forced to trade for something you need because you were not prepared, but if that happens then it is just a loss of your storage, not a profitable currency for you.

Chapter Seventeen

Communications

Communications is something that is important and yet overlooked for the most part.

In bad weather or any natural disaster, war, plagues, most every kind of a disaster, one or more of the electronic communications will work or come back online soon. But remember if we are hit with an EMP (**electromagnetic pulse)** bomb, nothing electronic will work. It will be a long time before any of it will work again. No phones, cars, electronics, computers, refigerators or generators will work. Even the Government cannot protect its own electronics when this type of disaster occurs. If you store your radios without the batteries inside them, the EMP will not damage them.

Incoming Communications:

When disaster strikes, one of the first things that you will need to know is just what is going on. In fact, depending on what happens, your best tool for survival may be the information you have regarding what is going on and what may be coming. We are lucky during this time in which we live. Many of our TVs, radios, phones and other forms of communication come to us from satellites. We don't have as many ground towers that can be damaged, so we have a better chance of maintaining communication than in the past, as well as maintaining communication from all around the world.

Many of the disasters that may come might be from bad weather, plague or financial collapse. Even in the event of a war in this day and age, you most likely will know it is coming and will have time to prepare or set into motion your plan to survive. It may only be a storm that you will want to ride out in your home, or as in Katrina, you may need to leave with your 72-hour kit. Having communication before, during and after an event is critical to your survival. Knowing what is coming may give you the advantage you will need to survive. One of the things that will cause panic is being out of touch with everyone, and fear is heightened when you don't know what is happening. You will need to know about the weather and how long before help may or may not arrive. To know it will be a long time before help is coming is better for you mentally than to not know what is going on. This is true even if it is going to be a long time. You can make plans and take inventory of your supplies and work out how to survive even if it is for an extended period of time.

Communication will also give you an idea as to how the people around you are doing. So the most important form of communication is with contact from the outside world, and most of all the authorities. You will need to know what is going on, when help is coming, when to go for food or help and when and where not to go. You can't be sure which form of communication will be working when disaster hits, so you will need a radio that will receive AM, FM, short-wave, Police, Military, Home Land Security, air planes, and local hand-held to cover all bases. There may not be power; the electrical grid may be down. If so, it is most likely to go down right at the beginning, and that is when you will need communication the most. You will need a radio that can run on more than one power supply or two or more radios. Your radio is so important that you should have at least two main radios. If one is damaged and you don't have a backup, you will be in the dark. I assure you that this will cause a panic in your group, and you may make a wrong decision that could cost you your life by making a decision without the proper information. You may go to the wrong place or at the wrong time and be placed in danger. The more up to date information you have, the better your chances are of survival.

Cabela's sells a good radio, Etón® Red Cross FR360 Emergency Radio. It costs about $50. There are many types of them out there. Most have all the radio bands. Some have flashlights built in them, and most have multi-power supplies. Most will run on AC or DC or solar and will have a hand crank. The cost is from $29 to $199. We have one in each of our 72-hour kits – one for each person.

Don't forget that even if the electrical grid is down, your car radio should work.

Two-way Communication:

The first thing to use is your cell phone. If you don't have one then you should get a pre-paid phone for each person in your group. It should be in their 72-hour bag. Remember, most of the pre-paid phones have service that is good for one year, so make sure you put the date on each phone and renew the service as needed.

Secondly, use your home phone. Have a list of people you need to contact beside the phone and the same list with each cell phone in each 72-hour bag.

Depending on the emergency, your On Star may work. It takes some time and money to take a class, but the class is easy to become a HAM operator. Each state's Homeland Security Department offers radio classes, and there are many local radio clubs that will have classes and sell radios. In the past, and I believe now and in the times to come, the HAM radio people will play a big and important role in communication during emergencies. HAMs can communicate all around the world. The radios cost around $1,000, but you may be able to contact people all around the world, and you don't have to know Morse code to use them anymore. We use hand-held HAM radios.

You can go to Wal-mart or a sporting goods store and buy at least two sets of the walkie-talkie. They cost from around $20 to $99. Most of these have twenty-two channels or more. They claim that walkie-talkies have up to a fifteen-mile range. This may be true in just the right conditions, but most of them will work for a mile or so. They are going to be good to use to keep in touch with your group, in your camp or your home. You may have people posted on upper floors keeping watch for other people or gangs, or you may need to go outside and wind up needing help yourself. HAMs will work from car to car if you are traveling. Some of the walkie-talkies have GPS built into them so you can locate your people. If they venture out and get hurt, you will be able to find them.

It may cost a great deal more money than most of you will want to spend, and most of you will not have a need for some of the things out there, but I will tell you about a few of them anyway. There are GPS units that snow skiers use so that if they are lost they can be tracked. These don't cost much, but you may not have a use for them because you should not allow your people to go too far on their own. We will teach you about patrolling in **Surviving A Hostile City II**.

Because we travel to war zones, we use a real time GPS tracking system. Each of us in the group wears one of these, and anyone who can get on the Internet and knows the password, can sit at the computer and locate each of us. We can keep track of each other from our vehicle or at our HQ, and our family back in the States can see where we are. If we get pinned down or are in a firefight, our quick response team can find and rescue us. This costs some money, and you have to have a working computer. The Internet has to be working, too. None of that may be working if a disaster hits in this country. However, if it is working, then this could be of great value to you.

<u>Other communications</u>:

Because we live in a high-tech world, we sometimes forget that there are simple things that not only work but also may be better than high-tech methods. The United States spent a million dollars to come up with a pen that will work in space with no gravity, but the Russians used a pencil. **Hand signals** are an example of this. You should practice hand signals. When you are close and don't want to make noise, this is what you should use. The Army has many hand signals, but you can make up your own as long as everyone in your group knows them.

Whistles; everyone in your group should carry a whistle and make up a list of signals everyone will know. Don't try to be too complicated, just make a few simple ones.

Mirrors; since the Old West, people have used mirrors to signal each other. It still works today. It not only works to signal one other, but you can use this method to signal a plane overhead. Signaling with a mirror can be seen for miles. Two things to remember about mirrors – you need sun to send the signal, and others will also be able to see your signal and know where you are. That may be bad, or you can use it to draw others into your trap. You can also start fires with a mirror (really hard to do).

Code words are important! If someone comes up to you, or you have to interact with others outside your group, codes words will help to keep you safe. Again, don't use too many code words or make them too complicated. You need a distress word that everyone will know. When someone is in trouble or is with someone and is being forced to bring him or her into your compound, you should have a distress word so you know there is something wrong. Make the signal a word that outside persons will not recognize as a signal. We like to use a code like having one of our people say, "it's okay," or "I'm ok." But when our person repeats "it's okay" and has said "it's okay" twice, then we know it is not okay. So, if he says, "I am okay, I really am okay," we know he is not okay. The bad guy should not catch on to your signal. More will be taught about this and how to deal with bad guys in **Surviving A Hostile City II**.

Passwords: Unlike you see in the movies, don't use the old style passwords. I remember watching old WW II movies where they would say "apple" and the password was pie. Don't use passwords like that. Not only could people guess what the password is, but also if they can get close enough to hear you, they can hear you say the password. The best way is to use a number that you change each day. For example, if the number for the day is 8, then when you see someone, you say any number that is 8 or smaller. The number they call back to you must add up to 8. So, if you say 4, then they would come back with 4 to equal 8.

Then you know they are okay. If you say 8 to the next person, then they should come back with 0 to add up to 8. You will know they are okay. This prevents the bad guys from repeating a password that they may have overheard. If you change numbers each day, and change what you call to each person, you will be okay.

Chapter Eighteen

Transportation

This book is mostly for people who live in large cities and towns. Some of you may live in apartments and not own your own vehicle. I hope you will use this book and learn to store food and supplies to be prepared. It is my recommendation that you stay in place if a disaster hits. You should only leave if for some reason you are forced to leave and only if you have a place ready to go, stocked with food, water and supplies. If not, please don't think about leaving.

You may have to leave because of natural disasters. In case you have to leave, you should keep your transportation in good running condition and full of fuel. Think about how large a truck you will need if you leave and take all your food, water and supplies with you. How much fuel would you need, and when you are out on the open road, remember you could be stopped by someone who will take what you have or even harm you.

If you stay where you are, there will come a time down the road when you will be alone in the city. That is the time when you could use some transportation to go scavenging. After all this time, a bicycle is still the most efficient mode of transportation. It uses less energy for the distance you travel. Most of all it doesn't use fuel that you will need for something else. Next you might consider buying a small motorcycle. It not only uses small amounts of fuel, but the streets will be full of trash and cars. It will be hard to get around in a car or truck. A motorcycle can go on sidewalks and lawns and places where a car cannot go.

Your vehicle should be in good shape and ready to go at all times before the disaster happens. But after a disaster occurs, then you need to stay in place and keep your vehicle safe from those people trying to find a way out of the city and from looters who in a few days will be trying to find anything they can use, your car or fuel or anything in it. You will have a hard time fighting looters; there will be too many of them. In **Surviving A Hostile City II** we will show you the best way to use your weapons to protect yourself and your supplies.

It is best to hide in plain sight. If you have a place in which to lock up your vehicle and keep it safe that's good, however, many people will not have a place to secure theirs. If you park in a parking garage then there will be many people who will have access to your vehicle. The looters will be going from place to place stealing everything in any car. So, this is what works best: take everything out of your vehicle, everything, don't give the looters a reason to break into it. Leave the trunk open with the spare tire and jack out of it. Leave your car unlocked and at least two windows rolled down so looters don't have to break the glass to see or get inside. Leave the glove box open with some papers that might normally be inside a glove box lying on the front seat and on the floor. Find some small (18 or 20 gauge) red and black wires and tape them under the dash so it appears as though someone has tried to hot wire your car. Leave only a gallon of fuel in the tank. Leave the gas tank lid open with a piece of hose hanging out, so looters will think someone has already taken the gas. You need to do this because most of them will not try to siphon your gas, they will simply put a pan under your tank and punch a hole in the tank. Leave some fuel, because most cars when they run out of gas, will not start after you add gas. Many cars have the fuel pumps in the fuel tanks, and if you run the car out of fuel entirely, this can damage your fuel pump.

Remember there will be public transportation around from which you may be able to obtain parts, and don't forget police cars will be around to steal from, as well.

Ask your friends and neighbors what they are going to do. You will find that most of them do not have a plan. Their first thought will be to leave, but they won't have supplies or a plan. I think you will see the wisdom of storing supplies and staying in place.

Chapter Nineteen

Nuclear-Chemical-Biological Attack

Nuclear:

In 1947, a group of scientists got together and set up a doomsday clock. It was meant to show how close we were to a nuclear war. This was right after the atomic bomb was used in WW II. The scientists set the clock at 11:53 p.m., or seven minutes until midnight. Midnight represents doomsday. The time has been changed over the years, and it is now set at six minutes before midnight. During the cold war everyone was worried about the Russians, but both the Russians and China are no longer the threat that they once were. In fact, the doomsday clock would be set back further from doomsday if Russia and China were the only threat. It is the threat from the small countries and terrorist groups that keeps the clock near midnight. A small suitcase bomb is the most likely threat at this time, as well as the threat of knowing that Iran would love to hit Israeli, which could start a global war. No matter who starts the war, the question is what can you do and how can you survive it?

If you are near ground zero when a nuclear bomb explodes, there is nothing you can do. Few people have a bomb shelter anymore, and most cities don't have one that could hold very many people or enough supplies to help people in a large city. There is little or nothing you can do to stop it from happening. There is nothing you can do to survive at or near the blast. If you live through the blast, then you may have a chance to survive. The best thing you can do is to have your food storage and be able to stay inside. Your survival is going to depend more on the weather, winds and where you are located in relation to ground zero.

You need to make your shelter as airtight as you can, don't go out, and don't eat or drink anything that has been exposed to the bomb and its fallout. Listen to the radio for information if you have a radio that functions. Unless you have a place to build shelter, and enough money, there is not much you can do. The best chance you have is to have your food and water storage and stay inside. That is also what you need to do to survive most of the disasters that may occur.

EMP:
This stands for Electromagnetic Pulse bomb. The Electro Magnetic Pulse is actually an electromagnetic shock wave. It is this aspect of the EMP effect, which is of military significance, as it can result in irreversible damage to a wide range of electrical systems and electronic equipment, particularly computers, radio or radar receivers. Subject to the electromagnetic hardness of the electronics, a measure of the equipment's resilience to this effect, and the intensity of the field produced by the weapon, the equipment can be irreversibly damaged, or in effect, electrically destroyed. The damage inflicted is not unlike that experienced through exposure to close proximity to lightning strikes, and may require complete replacement of the equipment, or at least substantial portions thereof.

Commercial computer equipment is particularly vulnerable to EMP effects, as it is largely built up of high-density Metal Oxide Semiconductor (MOS) devices, which are very sensitive to exposure to high voltage transients. Even if the pulse is not powerful enough to produce thermal damage, the power supply in the equipment will readily supply enough energy to complete the destructive process. Damaged devices may still function, but their reliability will be seriously impaired. Shielding electronics provides only limited protection, because any cables running in and out of the equipment will behave very much like antennas, guiding the high voltage transients into the equipment. You will not know if an EMP is coming, so there is not much you can do to stop it. Any electrical equipment you are currently using should have the batteries removed or be unplugged from the power supply in order to protect it. After the bomb goes off, anything you had hooked to a power supply will be damaged. Your best way to be prepared is to have extras of whatever equipment or devices you think you will need.

Chemical:
Some commercial chemicals are lethal. We are referring to nerve gases and lethal gases as utilized by the Military. These are hard to come by and hard to deliver to the target. Weather and wind degrade and disperse the chemicals very quickly. Therefore, the chance of you being hit with it is very small, but if you happen to be in the wrong place at the right time, then most likely you are going to die. In the Military, their best defense is their Intelligence that will warn them of a coming attack. They don't walk around wearing chemical gear. To be protected they have to wear a chemical-resistant suit, because most lethal gases are dermal (transfer though your skin). Military personnel have to have their gas

masks with them. Most lethal gases can't be seen or smelled, and only when someone goes down do you realize it is present. At that point you have to hold you breath, and you have about nine seconds to get your mask out, put it on, adjust it and clear it of the old air that is inside. This is hard for a well-trained soldier to do, let alone a civilian with no training. The filters only work one time and then they have to be changed. You will not find a good gas mask on the civilian market, and even if you buy one, you would need many filters and be sure to carry the mask at all times. Your best defense is to stay away from perennial targets, and again, have your food and water storage and stay in your home.

Some commercial gases are non-lethal. This category includes tear gases (CS) and pepper sprays. You may come into contact with them through contact with the police, military, gangs and Para-military units running the streets. You can go online and find some masks to help protect you from this form of gas. If the masks work well, then they will cost quite a bit of money. Only because of our military contacts were we able to store good chemical masks. Remember that even if you have a good mask and filters, they won't supply air to you. So, if you are in a place with low oxygen then the masks and filters will not help. Your best protection is again to stay inside. However, you can use some form of air tanks for protection. Scuba tanks carry their own air supply; if you go salvaging you should look for air masks and protective masks at fire stations. Also, search the city maintenance building; there should be both non-air and air masks and tanks used for working in underground and confined places. These will provide you with protection, but they are heavy and hard to carry around.

Then there are homemade gases. Don't be fooled into thinking that these are not lethal and pose no threat to you. In most homes, in the garage and under your sink, are chemicals that will kill or blind you. The biggest threat to you with homemade chemical weapons is going to be from the gangs and Para-military units. They will be using chemicals that they can throw in your face or spray on you. The important thing is to remember that you have the same resources as they do. In **Surviving A Hostile City II** we will provide detail about how to protect yourself and how to make and deliver homemade chemical weapons. For now, your best protection is to have food and water storage and stay in your home. I hope by now you can see how important having food storage and being able to stay inside is going to be for your survival. If you have your food storage then you will not need to read all the other chapters in this book including this one.

<u>Biological</u>:

Let's discuss natural biological disasters first such as plagues. A plague can occur when a disease that all races are subject to can spread over large areas. The Bubonic Plague in 1350 killed from 30 to 60% of the world population. Fleas that were living on rats carried the plague. The people at that time didn't know what the cause was and had no medicines to fight it, yet many survived. In this day and age we have medicines and know how Bubonic Plague is spread. We know that killing the fleas and rats would stop the spread of the disease.

There are also many natural diseases out there, but for the most part these are controlled by the use of vaccinations to prevent populations from coming down with the diseases. That is the key for you to survive: **Prevention!** You need to have yourself and everyone in your group vaccinated for all the major diseases for which there is a vaccination. Anthrax (six shots), Hepatitis A and B, Typhoid, Yellow Fever, Smallpox, (MMR) measles, mumps, rubella, and polio are some. Some of these vaccinations are good for life, but some require boosters. Some need to be taken every year like vaccines for influenza and pneumonia.

There are a few diseases that only sanitation and prevention on your part, by knowledge of how you become infected, is going to save you. For example, with HIV, there is no vaccination to prevent it. This is relayed by the exchange of body fluids. Body fluids are any fluid in your body that at some time comes in contact with your blood. Saliva is not a body fluid. A person with the HIV virus who spits on you will not necessarily infect you; his saliva doesn't come in contact with his blood supply in this manner. However, if the person has a cut in their mouth, the blood could come in contact with their saliva, so you can become infected because of the saliva.

During a disaster sanitation will be at it lowest, and you will be more at risk to be infected. Without running water and water becoming so valuable in order for you to stay alive, you will not be using water for sanitation like you do now day-to-day. Now you hopefully wash your hands every time you use the bathroom or get your hands dirty.

E-Coli (***Escherichia coli, commonly called food poisoning***) and Salmonella (**zoonotic disease**) will be a big problem. As we have traveled around the world in war zones or to natural disasters, these diseases have always been a big problem. There is no vaccination to prevent these diseases. Touching your face or lips after you have been in contact with the e-Coli easily spreads e-Coli. This could happen after you use the restroom or by touching something that someone else has touched who had the e-Coli bacteria on their hands. Salmonella is spread person-to-person by coming in contact with a contaminated person or animal or from a food source that is contaminated. Eggs are a good source of Salmonella. Cooking of eggs or meats at a high temperature, and making sure the food is cooked all the way through, will kill Salmonella. With both of these diseases, sanitation is the key to prevention. Because water will be in short supply, it is important to have in your storage large quantities of some type of hand sanitizer. Besides the ones that you can buy at the store that may cost more, not because they are more effective, but because they smell good or are not as hard on your skin, you can buy large amounts of rubbing alcohol. You can buy it in many of the dollar stores at a good price. You can also use bleach at a 10% solution, and it doesn't cost much. Both bleach and rubbing alcohol do a good job, but don't smell good and can be hard on your skin. Beer and liquor also contain alcohol and can be used. Gasoline will also work, but smells and is also hard on your skin. It will be in great demand, because no one will have enough gas following the disaster. There are many things in your garage or under your sink that contain alcohol or bleach; just read the labels and see which ones they are and compare the prices.

The above is not a complete list; you should consult your doctor and local health department about the health issues in your area. Also, read the chapter on medical for treatment. When out scavenging, auto parts stores have many products that will kill germs. These are items that most people will not take when they are looting.

Manmade Biological Disasters:

In this day and age the threat of a biological attack from terrorists is high. Someone who has been infected with Smallpox could board a plane in London, and there would not be any symptoms for hours. This person could fly to the U.S. and then just fly around the country going from city to city infecting everyone on the planes. Those infected in turn will infect everyone they come in contact with. Soon Smallpox would be spread all over the U.S. and anywhere else the infected people travel. The carrier would most likely die in a few days, but that person would be like the biggest suicide bomber there is, killing or infecting thousands of people.

In this country, we don't guard our water plants very well, and a terrorist could put something in the water or just drop a small amount of anthrax on a sidewalk in New York. This could kill thousands. In the U.S. it would have to be an agent that would infect all races to be effective. The United States is a mix of many races, and this may help us because terrorists would have to use an agent that would cross over racial lines.

The U.S. has biological weapons that are race specific so that they can introduce a virus and only affect a particular race. Other countries have these types of agents as well. Your best defense and prevention for a biological terrorist attack is again **Prevention!** Just as with the natural biological disaster, the same diseases will be the most likely to be used, so vaccinations are your best defense and hope for surviving a biological attack. Again, having your food storage so you can stay inside, and most of all, not have to come in contact with any outside sources of food that could be contaminated or with other people who may also be contaminated will be your best defense.

If you become contaminated and sicken then you will be in big trouble. You most likely will not have the medicines or medical skills to treat the problem, and you may also spread the disease to all the other people in your group.

Surviving a Hostile City V will be dedicated to nuclear, chemical and biological disasters.

Chapter Twenty

Cannibalism

This is the last chapter in the book. If you are reading this chapter because you need the information in it, then you are most likely in the last chapter of your life. You either didn't read the first part of this book, or you did but you did not act on the information and were not prepared for what was to come.

Unlike what you see in the movies about people killing people to eat and hunting them down or locking them in the basement to eat later, that is not what really happens. It would take food to feed the locked up people to keep them alive, or they would become sick and not be worth eating. They would need to consume food that you could eat.

Most people would turn to cannibalism only when all else has failed. Most of the time they are in a small group separated from others and have no way to obtain food or water. Most of the time they are lost at sea or in some hostile land area, or the weather has trapped them. They will only eat humans to say alive long enough to be rescued, not to live on for a long period of time. In the case of a national disaster and you are in a big city, it may be like being lost on an island. Most people will be gone or dead, and you will be alone without resources. Some civilizations eat their enemies or use humans as sacrifice and eat the heart or some part of them, but there is no recorded history about a civilization that lived on human flesh as part of their day-to-day diet.

Remember that there may be dead people around, but unless they are in a frozen state they will not be fit to eat in just a matter of hours. Body cells begin to break down within minutes of death. If you are going to eat human flesh, then it must be fresh meat. Eat only muscle and never the organs. In the past it was thought that the disease dies with the host, but we now know some viruses can live for hours after the person dies. Researchers have found live HIV virus in blood on tables that has been there for hours.

Most of us have heard of the Donner party that was trapped in the high mountains back in the winter of 1846. They ran out of food and in the end, ate the dead members of their party. It was cold, so the meat lasted a long time, but many of the people died because they just couldn't eat humans. More would have survived if they had eaten humans earlier. They wrote the person's last name on the meat so that they didn't have to eat someone in their family. It did save lives, but they only resorted to this drastic measure because they had to survive until help came.

Following some disasters or catastrophic events, you are not going to be in the same position as the Donner party. No one is going to come to your rescue. There will be dead around, street people, but most of them will have some type of disease and are not fit to eat. The reality is that to find fresh edible human beings is going to be hard. Most people will starve rather then eat humans. If you come to a point when you are down to eating humans, you will be at the lowest physical and emotional point in your life and most likely not survive anyway without outside assistance.

Web Sites for Training, Gear and Supplies:

pipehitterstactical.com

preparednessdeals.com

pipehittersgear.com

tacticalbootcamo.com

survivalcorner.com

Food Storage Site:

longlifefood.com

E-mail Addresses:

kaalwood@hotmail.com

lornadare@live.com

Appendix A
72-Hour Supplies

<u>72-hour Kit Bag</u>:
- Store your supplies in a bag that you can **grab and go** with.
- Don't put more than one person's supplies in one bag; each person should have their own bag, even a small child. That way it is easy to keep track of what each person needs. Each person's needs vary as to age, sex, size and health.
- Allow each person to help and have a "say" in preparing his or her own 72-hour kit.
- Put a tag on the kit with a date and check it once a year. Change out food that may only have a year storage life. Doing this each New Year's will help you to remember.
- If you are taking medicine, you will not be able to store it in the bag until you are ready to go, so leave yourself a note on the bag as a reminder to put your meds in the bag before you leave. Use red paper to catch your attention.

<u>Clothing</u>:
- Think about where you live. If you live in Texas you will need different clothing than someone who lives in Michigan.
- Remember, this is only for 72 hours or three days, and you are not going to a fashion show. Pick clothing for the weather conditions and for practicality.
- Pack clothing for the worst conditions.
- Remember to check you clothes once a year, and if you have children who are still growing you will need to keep changing their clothes to meet their needs as they grow.
- It is best to pack the clothes in waterproof bags to insure they will be clean and dry when you need them.
- Remember that you may have to carry your 72-hour bag a long way, so don't over pack. If you have small children you will have to carry their bag also.
- If you have children in diapers, you will have to carry or transport them and have diapers and infant supplies.

<u>Food/Water</u>:

- Foods need to be lightweight, compact and need no refrigeration or cooking.
- Keep in mind you could go without food for 72 hours. So don't over pack.
- Pack foods high in energy and low in weight.
- Keep in mind the age, needs and personal likes of each person.
- Don't pack food that you don't normally eat. People will do without rather than eat food they don't like.
- If you find food you have never eaten and think it would be good for your kit, **try it before you pack it.** Always try a new food to make sure you like it.
- Keep in mind the weight of the food, and remember it has to store for at least a year.
- You should change most of the food out once a year.
- Eat what you change out so it doesn't go to waste.
- Store food somewhere where there are not extremes in heat and cold.
- MRE's provide protein and energy, store a long time and are easy to carry.
- Protein is always the hardest thing to store and costs the most per ounce.
- Cans of tuna and packages of jerky are good forms of protein to pack.
- Hard candy gives a great deal of energy and doesn't take up much space.
- Bottled water needs to be stored in your bag to be ready to go. Remember to store the kit where it will not freeze.
- Don't forget foods for your pets.
- Pack formula and baby food for small children.

<u>Medical Supplies</u>:

- First-Aid Book or Manual
- Standard first-aid kit, one for each person.
- Insect bite medications
- Medications. Remember if you need your meds on a day-to-day basis, so you will not store them in the kit. Make yourself a note to remind yourself to put them in your bag before you leave.

- Aspirin & Ibuprofen
- Chap stick, sun block
- Extra glasses
- Alcohol Wipes
- Chlorine Bleach

Equipment:
- Hand-operated Can Opener
- Whistle
- Multi-powered Radio
- Batteries
- Flashlight, extra Batteries
- Disposable Plates, Cups & Utensils
- Cell Phone and Hand-cranked Charger
- Fire Extinguisher
- Maps
- Pen, Pencil, Paper
- Light Sticks
- Candles
- All-Weather Blankets
- Sleeping Bag
- Leatherman, Multi-use tool
- If there is more than one of you, small two-way radios and batteries.

Personal Items:
- Toilet Paper
- Soap, Liquid and/or Bar
- Toothbrush & Paste
- Comb or Brush
- Razor
- Feminine Hygiene Items
- Diapers and anything the Baby needs

Currency:
- Change to make calls
- Cash in small denominations: $1 - $5 - $10
- Phone cards
- Silver, in one-ounce units

Personal Protection Items:
Remember that when you leave your home, you will be in a more vulnerable position. It is up to you to decide if you wish to take weapons. Also, you need to check and know your local laws about what is and is not legal in your area. Go to the chapter on weaponry to see details on the items listed below:

- Pepper Spray
- Stun Guns
- Handgun
- Rifle
- Ammo
- Knifes, Multi-Function Pocket Knife
- Bow and Arrow
- Pellet Gun

Entertainment:
It is important to have something to do to occupy your time if you are relocated or in your home and there is no power for your TV and other forms of entertainment. You and your friends or family will be under a great deal of stress, and it will only add to your stress if all you can do is sit around to talk and complain about your situation.

You may have power where you go. If so, then you can take a portable CD's, DVD's and laptops. Think about what you can do if there is no power such as play board games, cards, puzzles. Games that require you to have physical activity like horseshoes and Hobo Golf are good because physical activity helps reduce stress.

The list above may contain more than you need, or it may contain less. It is up to you to decide. What will suit your life style and your location?

Just remember you can't eat your insurance policy when you are out of food. FEMA and the Red Cross are not going to be there to take care of you, and it could be like what occurred in New Orleans when most of the police went home to take care of their families leaving the citizens to fend for themselves.

Appendix B
Food Storage Items

Protein:

Canned or dried – bacon – beef – beef jerky – chicken – clams – corned beef – crabmeat – fish – ham – hamburger – lamb – pepperoni – pork – tuna – sandwich meats – Spam – turkey – venison jerky.

The first thing people will be without is protein (meat). I have been all over the world, and protein is always the problem when you are gathering food on your own. There have been times when I had lots of carbohydrates, but I needed protein. I have eaten dogs, cats, rats, snakes, lizards, monkeys and about everything you can think of.

Protein that will store for a year is what you should look to store. Protein is going to be the biggest expense on your food storage list. Here are some ideas: soups, chicken, beef stews, clam chowder, jerky and other dehydrated meats.

Grains**:**

Barley – cereal – flour – oats – popcorn – rye – wheat – rice.

You can store flour, but it doesn't last a year without being placed in a container that is sealed and has no oxygen inside. You can do so much with flour such as make breads, pancakes, cakes and many other baked goods, and it doesn't cost much. You can buy flour sealed and ready for storage from many places on the web. You can use 5-gallon plastic buckets for storage. Place a liner in the bucket and put the flour in the bags. Before you seal the bag, place an oxygen absorber inside and then seal it. Then put another oxygen absorber inside and seal the 5-gallon bucket with the lid.

http://survivalacres.com/information/oxygen_absorbers-info.htm. Go to this site to learn about oxygen absorbers and to purchase them.

Rice can be stored the same way and is good for long periods of time.

Make up a list of meals or things you are going to make with your grains. Then make a list of all the other ingredients you will need to turn you flour into breads or pancakes or whatever it is you wish to make. Flour alone is not very good.

Vegetables:
Pinto beans – white beans– sprouting beans – soybeans – asparagus – beets – broccoli – Brussels sprouts – carrots – cauliflower – celery – sweet corn – hominy – mushrooms – onions – peas – peppers – pickles – flaked potatoes – pumpkins – rutabagas – sauerkraut – spinach – yams – tomatoes.

There are many kinds of vegetables out there, and most are available in cans that will store for a year or longer.

Fruits:
Apples – applesauce – apricots – peaches – cherries – coconut – fruit cocktail – grapefruit – oranges – olives – pears – peaches – pineapples – plums – raisins.

Most fruits come in cans and store well for a year. They are also a good source of sugar.

Milk:
Brick cheese – canned milk – canned sour cream – cheese spreads – condensed milk – dried cheeses – dried eggs – non-dairy creamer – non-fat dry milk – powdered cheese.

Milk products add to you storage. To make pancakes and many other dishes, you need to store powdered milk. Also think about powered eggs. Those are products that have a high cost, but will be so important in the end. Most of those products come in some kind of a cardboard container. I recommend that you put them in a plastic pail with a lid that seals, and use the oxygen absorbers.

Sugar:
Corn syrup – hard candy – honey – maple syrup – molasses – puddings – sugar.

Sugar comes in many forms, doesn't cost much and stores well. You can store cans of pie filling. These are great on pancakes or rice.

Sugar comes most of the time in a paper bag and will absorb moisture. However, unless it is contaminated, it will last a long time. Even if it turns hard from the moisture, all you have to do is break off a piece, and it is good. However, again, if you store it in some kind of plastic container and use oxygen absorbers, it will store a long time. This is something you can store in large amounts. Store more than you think you will need. When people are out of food, sugar, coffee, and proteins become currency as well as food. Don't forget that honey is just sugar, is easy to store and lasts a long time.

Spices:
Allspice – baking chocolate – baking soda – Basil – BBQ sauce – bouillon cubes – celery salt – chili powder – chives – chocolate chips – chocolate syrup – cinnamon – cloves – cocoa – cumin – dill – garlic salt – ginger – gravy mixes – ketchup – lemon juice – maple extract – nutmeg – onion salt – oregano – pepper – sage – salt – seasoned salt – soy sauce – vanilla extract – vinegar – Worcestershire sauce.

Don't forget about spices and all the little things that make your food taste the way you like it and are needed to make other foods. I can't tell you everything you will personally need because everyone cooks with different spices and ingredients.

Look over the recipes you use and add all the little things you need into your storage.

Oils:
Butter – cooking oils – lard – margarine – mayonnaise – peanut butter – salad dressing – shortening.

Don't forget the cooking oils. Most of them are in some type of plastic bottle and will store for a year. Again, I can't tell you which ones to buy – buy what you use.

Drinkable Water/Juices:
Apple juice – apricot juice – cocoa drink mix – cranberry juice – dried juice mixes – grapefruit – grape juice – Kool Aid – lemonade – orange juice – pineapple juice – prune juice – soft drink mixes – tomato juice – V-8 juice.

Depending on where you live, water may be one of the biggest items you will have to store. Bottled water is the best and easiest to store. Powered Gatorade, or whatever you like, is good to store. You can add this to your water and increase your electrolytes.

Soda is sometimes cheaper than water at Wal-mart or other stores.

Don't forget there is water in your water heater and your waterbed. If you have a warning before the disaster hits and enough time, you can fill your tub.

The above are items you will most likely have to buy; they are not things you will be able to go out and obtain in some other way.

Supplemental Foods:
Baking powder – baking soda – cake mixes – casserole mixes – noodles – cookies – cornstarch – crackers – hot roll mixes – instant breakfast – iron supplements – marshmallows – MRE's (meals ready to eat) – pet foods – pancake mixes – pastry mixes – pie crust mixes – pie fillings – pizza mixes – survival bars – vitamins.
These items are very important, because they will add variety in your meals.

On the Cover:

Lorna Dare
Kent Alwood

Officer R. Tom Robison
Fremont, IN Police Department

Bruce DeLucenay

Ron Kauffman

Bill Bryan

Lonnie L. Mills

Dan Hensell

Cover Photograph by:

Joseph L. McClure
260-744-9451

A special thanks to
Kelly Alwood.
Kelly will be a Co-author for our next book,
Surviving a Hostile City II –
Defensive and Offensive Tactics

Thanks also to the following people for their help with the book:

Max Frielander

Dennis Marcello

Ron Kauffman